"This book is a must-read for any new teacher. I w[…]
[s]upport before I started teaching!"

—JIL[…]

"Thompson's work helps beginning teachers—even those with no prior teaching
[e]xperience—to understand the basics of effective teaching. *The First-Year Teacher's
[C]hecklist* makes it easy for educators who are just starting out to understand what
[i]t will take to become a successful teacher. I will definitely make this book required
[r]eading for my teacher interns."

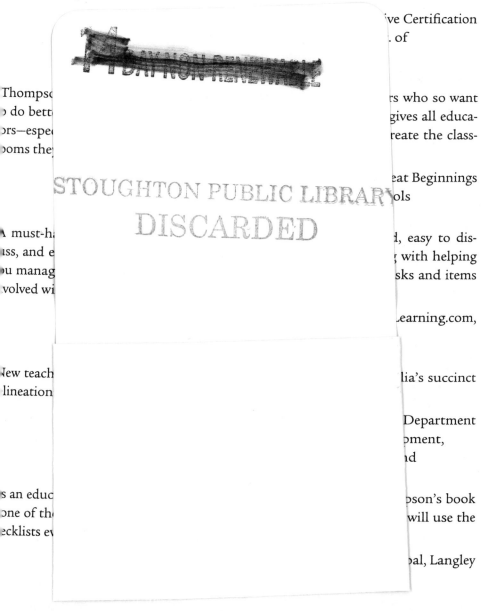

[…]ve Certification
[…]. of

Thomps[…]   [teache]rs who so want
[t]o do bett[…]   gives all educa-
[t]ors—espe[…]   [c]reate the class-
[r]ooms the[…]

[Gr]eat Beginnings
[…]ols

[A] must-h[…]   [an]d, easy to dis-
[cu]ss, and e[…]   [g] with helping
[yo]u manag[…]   [ta]sks and items
[in]volved wi[…]

[…]Learning.com,

[N]ew teach[…]   [Ju]lia's succinct
[de]lineation[…]

[…]Department
[…][devel]opment,
[…]d

[A]s an educ[…]   [Thom]pson's book
[…]one of th[…]   will use the
[ch]ecklists ev[…]

[…]al, Langley

"Completely comprehensive, *The First-Year Teacher's Checklist* provides easy-to-find, concise suggestions for any situation facing a new teacher. Judy Thompson's advice is on point, providing a clear framework for all new teachers to follow while at the same time providing a path for them to explore their individual teaching styles and grow into their new profession."

—STEVE PLUNKETT, Humanities department
chair, Langley High School, McLean, VA

JOSSEY-BASS TEACHER

Jossey-Bass Teacher provides educators with practical knowledge and tools to create a positive and lifelong impact on student learning. We offer classroom-tested and research-based teaching resources for a variety of grade levels and subject areas. Whether you are an aspiring, new, or veteran teacher, we want to help you make every teaching day your best.

From ready-to-use classroom activities to the latest teaching framework, our value-packed books provide insightful, practical, and comprehensive materials on the topics that matter most to K–12 teachers. We hope to become your trusted source for the best ideas from the most experienced and respected experts in the field.

The Jossey-Bass Web site features free downloadable study guides that accompany this book: one is for individual teachers using *The First-Year Teacher's Checklist* with their classroom work; another is for staff developers using this book in in-service workshops. To access these free study guides, go to **www.josseybass.com/go/thompsonchecklist.**

The First-Year Teacher's Checklist

A Quick Reference for Classroom Success

JULIA G. THOMPSON

JOSSEY-BASS
A Wiley Imprint
www.josseybass.com

371.1
Tho

Published by Jossey-Bass
A Wiley Imprint
989 Market Street, San Francisco, CA 94103-1741—www.josseybass.com

Jossey-Bass books and products are available through most bookstores. To contact Jossey-Bass
directly, call our Customer Care Department within the U.S. at 800-956-7739, outside the U.S.
at 317-572-3986, or fax 317-572-4002.

Jossey-Bass also publishes its books in a variety of electronic formats. Some content that
appears in print may not be available in electronic books.

Library of Congress Cataloging-in-Publication Data
Thompson, Julia G.
    The first-year teacher's checklist : a quick reference for classroom success / Julia G.
Thompson.—1st ed.
        p. cm.— (Jossey-Bass teacher)
    Includes index.
    ISBN 978-0-470-39004-7 (pbk.)
    1. First year teachers.   2. Teacher orientation.   3. Teaching.   I. Title.
LB2844.1.N4T515   2009
371.1—dc22
                                                                    2008041898

Printed in the United States of America
FIRST EDITION
PB Printing   10 9 8 7 6 5 4 3 2 1

Dedication

For Phil, with gratitude, admiration, and love

Contents

SECTION FOUR   **LOOK TO THE FUTURE**   **163**

Chapter 12   **Twenty-First Century Issues for All Teachers**   **165**

SECTION FIVE   **HELPFUL RESOURCES FOR EDUCATORS**   **179**

Chapter 13   **Resources to Help You Become a Better Teacher**   **181**

About This Book

In every school, beginning teachers are the busiest and most easily overwhelmed employees. Not only do they have to accomplish the same tasks with the same degree of proficiency as their experienced colleagues, but their unfamiliar responsibilities are often daunting.

The First-Year Teacher's Checklist was written expressly for you, a new teacher, pressed for time, who needs immediate answers, ideas, techniques, and teaching tools. You'll find that each topic in the book is addressed in the form of a brief, easy-to-read list. Each list provides you with the most important ideas or highlights on the topic under study. This practical format makes it easy for you to make swift, informed decisions about your teaching practices.

You will be able to quickly locate solutions to some of your immediate problems and save time spent searching for current resources on topics that are at the forefront of educational research. This book also provides teacher-tested advice on how to develop positive relationships with your students and colleagues, as well as how to design and deliver effective instruction and assessments. The quick support and guidance within these lists will help you make the right decisions to transform your classroom into an orderly, productive environment in which you and your students can work and learn together successfully.

About the Author

Best-selling author Julia G. Thompson has been a public school teacher for more than twenty-five years. She has taught a wide variety of subjects, including English, reading, special education, math, geography, home economics, physical education, and employment skills. Her students have ranged from reluctant seventh graders to gifted college students. Thompson currently teaches English in Fairfax County, Virginia, and she is an active speaker and consultant. Author of *The First-Year Teacher's Survival Guide* and *Discipline Survival Kit for the Secondary Teacher,* she also publishes a Web site that offers tips for teachers on a wide variety of topics. To learn more, go to www.juliagthompson.com.

Acknowledgments

I am especially grateful to my editor, Marjorie McAneny, for her insight, enthusiasm, hard work, and patience during the preparation of this book.

Thanks to two extraordinarily gifted teachers, Luann Scott and Charlene Herrala, for their astute advice about what new teachers really need.

Special thanks to the readers who take the time to write e-mails that share their encouraging stories about how to survive that all-important first year of teaching.

Introduction

FEW FORCES OF NATURE can equal a dedicated teacher. We spend our days focused on educating every child entrusted to our care, fully aware of the dire consequences should we fail. We do this without enough hours in the day to accomplish even part of our workload, but we still go to class each day determined to make a difference in the lives of our students.

How do we do it all?

We spend countless hours juggling tedious paperwork; designing engaging, challenging instruction; and empowering our students not just to be proficient test takers but to be educated, successful adults. We listen, we ask questions, we entertain, we laugh, we nurture, and we develop our students' minds. We give the world a future.

Because teachers are always pressed for time, we are always searching for ways to make our job more efficient, more manageable, more successful. We need ways to make our school days easier and more enjoyable.

The First-Year Teacher's Checklist was written to provide you with a quick overview of some of the most important issues confronting new teachers today. In this book you will be able to find what you need to know quickly because information has been condensed into brief lists that cover fundamental topics and provide answers to vital questions about the practicalities of running a classroom.

In each of the five sections of the book you will find lists of suggestions, ideas, and tips that highlight the material under study. The lists will provide you with easy-to-read information on how to develop your professional expertise, create a positive classroom culture, become a dynamic teacher, acquaint yourself with some of the newest trends in education, and learn how to find more information about each topic. *The First-Year Teacher's Checklist*'s main goals are to do the following:

1. Make it easy for you to find quick answers to the many questions about practical matters you may have as you begin your career

2. Keep you up to date with information and resources that will help you learn about the current trends in education and their impact on your classroom

3. Help you develop productive professional relationships with colleagues, students, their families, and supervisors

4. Allow you to use your time and resources wisely as you arrange your classroom and begin to establish classroom routines for yourself and your students

5. Offer advice and support about the most effective instructional practices that can allow to you design, deliver, and access instruction that is appropriate and meaningful to all of your students

Section One: Become a Professional Educator

CHAPTER ONE: How to manage your professional responsibilities and develop your career skills

CHAPTER TWO: How to cultivate successful work relationships with your colleagues

CHAPTER THREE: How to reach out to the parents and guardians of your students so that you can work together to make the school year a successful one for your students

Section Two: Create a Positive Class Culture

CHAPTER FOUR: How to set up your classroom for maximum comfort and learning

CHAPTER FIVE: How to make a positive connection with each of your students

CHAPTER SIX: How to motivate your students to become independent learners

CHAPTER SEVEN: How to use proven strategies that will prevent misbehavior

CHAPTER EIGHT: How to handle misbehavior so that disruptive effects are minimal

Section Three: Be a Dynamic Teacher

CHAPTER NINE: How to design instruction that will appeal to every student

CHAPTER TEN: How to deliver engaging, appropriate instruction using classroom-tested strategies, activities, and techniques

CHAPTER ELEVEN: How to assess your students' progress and thrive in the world of high-stakes testing

Section Four: Look to the Future

CHAPTER TWELVE: How to successfully meet some of the challenges in education that are common at the start of the twenty-first century

Section Five: Helpful Resources for Educators

You will find an extensive list of the most popular and helpful books, Web sites, and professional organizations available to teachers.

CHAPTER THIRTEEN: How to find the tools, information, and advice you need to accomplish a variety of tasks such as working well with others, setting up and managing a classroom, and developing your career

CHAPTER FOURTEEN: How to use the books and Web sites that can help you forge strong relationships with students and assist struggling learners

Busy teachers can use the practical, teacher-friendly lists in this book in many ways. You can browse through the book section by section, highlighting the ideas and approaches that best fit your classroom situation. Or you can check for specific information about a topic you need to know about at the moment. However you choose to use this book, the most effective purpose is to enable you and your students to enjoy a successful, productive learning environment.

Best wishes for a wonderful school year!

February 2009

Julia G. Thompson
Langley High School
Fairfax County, Virginia

To learn more about how you can have a successful school year, visit the author at **www.juliagthompson.com**.

Section One

Become a Professional Educator

Becoming a professional educator involves more than just lesson plans, grading papers, and high-stakes testing. In this section, you'll learn the importance of professional development, how to form working relationships with your colleagues, and how to work as a team with the parents or guardians of your students.

IN CHAPTER ONE, you'll have the opportunity to learn about the many methods that you can use to develop into the competent educator you would like to be. You'll learn workplace skills as well as how to conduct yourself as a confident professional educator capable of successfully fulfilling your responsibilities, managing your stress, and meeting the expectations of those around you.

IN CHAPTER TWO, the emphasis is on how you can become a valuable member of the team of teachers and other staff members at your school. You'll learn the importance of developing beneficial, supportive, and enjoyable relationships with your colleagues as well as strategies that you can use to build those important relationships.

IN CHAPTER THREE, the focus is on how you can make the crucial connection between home and school into a positive one for your students, their families, and yourself. You'll learn why this relationship is important and various strategies that will make it easier to establish a productive bond.

CHAPTER 1

Professional Development Begins with You

1-1 Be Guided by the Principles of Professionalism

Great teachers are defined by the extent of their dedication to developing the attitudes, knowledge, and skills that are the hallmarks of a professional educator. As you begin to develop your career, let the following principles of professionalism guide your efforts:

* **PRINCIPLE ONE:** Commit yourself to the well-being and success of every student in your care.

    + Treat all students with dignity and respect.

    + Honor your students by having high expectations for their academic and behavioral success.

    + Maintain an organized and orderly classroom where students are kept safe from harm.

    + Promote positive behaviors that aid the development of self-efficacy.

* **PRINCIPLE TWO:** Commit yourself to maintaining rigorous standards of professional performance.

    + Accept responsibility for what happens in your classroom.

    + Conduct your professional life with impeccable integrity.

    + Initiate a teamwork approach to a successful school year with the parents and guardians of your students.

    + Recognize that the constantly changing complexity of education makes professional growth a personal responsibility.

* **PRINCIPLE THREE:** Commit yourself to delivering the most appropriate instruction for your students.

    + Differentiate instruction to meet the individual needs of all learners.

    + Help students set and achieve reasonable goals based on state standards.

    + Be aware of and incorporate educational best practices.

    + Provide written and verbal feedback designed to encourage student achievement.

1-2   What Is Expected of You

Although expectations vary from school to school, here is a list of some of the expectations that other teachers, your students, your supervisors, and the parents or guardians of your students will have of you as you begin your new career. You will be expected to

* Design instruction that appeals to the various learning modalities of your students
* Use state standards to inform instruction
* Demonstrate knowledge of your students' development, skills, abilities, and aptitudes
* Help students establish and achieve learning goals
* Understand how students learn and use that knowledge to reach your students
* Differentiate instruction so that the individual needs of all learners are met
* Use sound judgment about which teaching practices are suitable for your students
* Establish a positive relationship with every student
* Treat all students with dignity and respect regardless of factors such as ethnicity or gender
* Use a variety of methods to motivate students to perform well in school both academically and behaviorally
* Use technology to enhance your instructional practices
* Establish a safe and productive classroom environment
* Use techniques that minimize the loss of time on task when disruptions occur
* Provide a risk-free and supportive learning environment
* Administer appropriate assessments to determine student mastery levels
* Assume responsibility for your own professional growth
* Work collaboratively with colleagues for the benefit of all staff members and students

* Professional growth does not happen by chance. Take charge by developing a personal plan to improve your teaching skills.

* Although you will almost certainly be assigned an official mentor, other teachers can also serve as role models. Look to them for support, inspiration, and advice.

* In addition to teachers in your building, form relationships with colleagues outside your school. Professional organizations and online educational forums are good places to begin building a professional network.

* Set career goals for yourself, and work to achieve them.

* Read materials that will keep you informed about current issues, trends, and techniques.

* Learn what the No Child Left Behind Act requires of all teachers.

* Join professional organizations related to your teaching assignment. Try to attend a conference sponsored by a professional organization, too.

* Take advantage of professional development opportunities such as workshops, webinars, online courses, and seminars offered by your school district.

* Keep a professional portfolio so that you will be able to measure your own growth as a teacher as the year progresses.

* Try to observe other teachers as often as you can. Ask them to observe you and offer their insights about your teaching performance.

* Make a plan to manage your stress levels so that you can avoid burnout.

* Investigate the National Board for Professional Teaching Standards. Many school districts now assist teachers who enroll in this program.

1-4 Set Professional Goals with These Easy Steps

A goal-oriented approach to your new career will help clarify your thinking, make the challenging task of professional development manageable, and make decision making easier all year long.

* **STEP ONE:** Set aside time to brainstorm about what you would like to learn, the obstacles you need to overcome, and how you can improve your teaching skills this year.

* **STEP TWO:** Select the most important ideas in your list and express them as long-range goals you would like to achieve.

* **STEP THREE:** Examine your long-range plans closely to make sure that they answer these questions for successful goals:

  + Are they productive? Will they help you develop professional skills?

  + Are they specific? Do they address a definite purpose or area that you would like to improve?

  + Are they measurable? Can you measure progress so that you will know when you have achieved them?

  + Are they achievable? Can you accomplish them with consistent, focused effort?

  + Are they timely? Do they have a time frame to keep you focused?

* **STEP FOUR:** Create short-term goals that complement your long-range goals by deciding on the specific steps that you must take to accomplish them.

* **STEP FIVE:** Write out your goals in detail, making sure to set benchmarks to track your progress. Find a place to keep them where they can serve as a reminder of what you want to accomplish this year.

1-5 Develop a Professional Demeanor

* Always be on time to school, to extracurricular duties, to meetings, and to class.

* Dress in a professional manner. Your clothing should project the image of a dignified, capable adult.

* Communicate in a mature manner: speak Standard English, avoid excessive slang, proofread what you write, and never curse at school.

* Be knowledgeable about your school district's policies and procedures.

* Follow school rules, policies, and directions from supervisors. If you disagree with a rule, follow the proper channels to change it.

* Exhibit self-control. Learn from constructive criticism and your own mistakes.

* Have a thorough knowledge and understanding of the content that you teach.

* Actively seek to learn more about current best teaching practices in your field.

* Be organized and efficient about how you manage your time, workload, and classroom.

* Convey your pride in your profession and your interest in being the best teacher that you can be.

* Be appreciative of your colleagues' experience and expertise.

* Demonstrate that you understand and value the importance of teamwork at school.

* Take a mature, mutually supportive approach to your relationships with the parents or guardians of your students.

* Be friendly to your colleagues, community members, students, and their families.

* Manage your anxiety levels with sensible stress reduction techniques.

* Become a lifelong learner about your subject matter, students, and career.

* Use school resources wisely. For example, you should turn off lights, keep track of textbooks, use the heating and air conditioning systems efficiently, and save paper.

* Share the photocopier courteously. Don't make others wait while you copy hundreds of handouts.

* Clean up after yourself.

* If you borrow something from another teacher, return it promptly and in good condition.

* Cultivate good telephone and e-mail manners.

* Develop exemplary time management skills. Use a planning calendar and a list of prioritized chores on a daily basis.

* Learn to use educational software and technological resources efficiently.

* Create a well-organized work space. Be sure to leave your desk clean at the end of the day.

* Be meticulous about keeping paperwork organized and up to date.

* Keep a file of ideas for lessons, activities, and other strategies that you would like to try.

* Arrive at school a little early, and leave a little late.

* Look ahead! Plan your lessons and activities far enough in advance that you don't have to scramble to carry them out.

* Learn to manage stress and the pressures of each day.

* Be flexible when your plans don't work out or when interruptions disrupt a lesson.

* Learn the art of taking control of your time. Volunteer for activities you can manage well, and politely decline those that you can't.

* Resist the urge to complain. Remaining cheerful under stress is an invaluable workplace skill.

* Create an electronic "To-Do List" template that shows routine chores. Print it, and use it to prioritize and schedule your work.

* Create routines to make your workdays predictable and manageable.

* Ask your colleagues for suggestions when you create lesson plans. They may have plans, worksheets, activities, or other ideas to share with you.

* Research on the Internet for lesson ideas, worksheets, and other helpful time-savers.

* Do a task right the first time so that you don't have to redo it.

* If you can, share a time-consuming task with colleagues; you will save time, learn from their experience, and have fun, too.

* Write down things you will need to remember.

* Plan how you will use your planning time at school. If you don't plan, those brief moments will slip away.

* Avoid the impulse to aimlessly chat with colleagues instead of working productively in your spare time at school.

* Break a large task into smaller, manageable ones.

* Learn to schedule your most challenging work at the times of day when your energy is high.

* Use small blocks of time. You can accomplish a lot in just a few minutes.

* If you don't understand something, ask. If you need help, ask.

* Keep your work area uncluttered and organized so that you don't have to search for misplaced items.

* Don't overextend yourself.

* No matter how busy you are, take a moment to enjoy your students.

1-8   How to Use Best Practices in Your Classroom

As a new teacher, you have probably heard the term *best practices* many times in your education courses, but you may not be sure what it means or what constitutes educational best practices. While there is no clear-cut definition of the term as it relates to education, most educators would agree that best practices are the actions that teachers can take to ensure that their instruction is effective, appropriate, and productive. Following is a list of some of the classroom-tested activities that qualify as educational best practices:

* Cooperative learning
* Portfolio assessments
* Alternative assessments
* Rubrics
* Tiered instruction
* Scaffolding instruction
* Anchoring activities
* Graphic organizers
* Essential questions
* Project-based learning
* Student-directed learning
* Workshop approaches to reading and writing
* Interdisciplinary instruction
* Inquiry-based instruction
* Authentic experiences
* Data-driven instruction
* Integrated technology
* Standards-based curriculums
* Benchmark testing
* Capitalizing on background knowledge
* Differentiated instruction
* Recognizing learning styles
* Recognizing multiple intelligences
* Teacher as coach and facilitator
* Student research

* Obtain copies of your district's evaluation forms so that you can become thoroughly familiar with the process and the expectations that observers will have for your performance.

* Talk with your peers, your mentor, and your supervisors to ask for advice that will ensure a successful observation and evaluation.

* On the day of the evaluation, be prepared.

    + Use excellent lesson plans that showcase your teaching skills.

    + Provide a place for the evaluator to sit as well as copies of all handouts.

    + Prepare students for the visit, and make sure your room is tidy.

* Don't wait until an administrator is in your room to be observed. Ask several colleagues to observe you at various times and offer feedback on your performance.

* In addition to arranging for collegial observations, make a point of periodically observing other teachers.

* Learn to use "snapshots" to evaluate your own expertise, prepare for formal evaluations, and grow professionally. Here's how:

    + Focus on just a few minutes of class time. During this time, unobtrusively audiotape or videotape yourself.

    + As you review the tape, evaluate specific behaviors. For example, a snapshot can be particularly useful for judging how you handle off-task behavior or give directions.

    + Keep a record of your insights, and use them to create the small improvements that will result in a formal observation that showcases your strengths.

* Take a sensible approach to your new profession. When you are having a bad day, remember that other teachers have experienced similar problems and may be able to offer help.

* Adopt a problem-solving approach when difficulties arise. When you do, you will be working toward a solution instead of just being miserable.

* Use the problems that you experience as opportunities to learn and become a better teacher. Don't dwell on your mistakes. Learn from them instead.

* Refuse to take it personally when a student or difficult colleague is rude, stressed out, or uncooperative.

* Plan some time to relax. Learn to schedule small moments to pause and recharge throughout your day.

* Keep problems small. Solve them as quickly and efficiently as possible to keep them from adding to your stress.

* Keep things in perspective by asking, "Will this matter a year from now?"

* Do routine tasks as efficiently as possible to avoid falling behind in your responsibilities.

* Learn to anticipate and appreciate the small successes that constitute a teacher's day. Celebrate with your students as often as you can.

* Even the very best teachers can't reach every child every day. Be realistic about what you can and can't accomplish.

* Take it one day at a time.

* Reward yourself occasionally when you have accomplished a difficult task at school.

* Leave your problems at school, but take your successes home.

* Have a thorough knowledge of the content that you are required to teach. Look ahead, and become familiar with the entire scope of your course.

* Create a course overview so that you know when you are supposed to cover various topics and are able to plan with assurance.

* Prepare your lessons as far in advance as you can. Even if you have to change plans or adjust due dates, you will still feel in control of your lesson preparation.

* Develop a sense of humor about your mistakes.

* Dress the part. Invest in comfortable professional clothes so that you do not have to worry about your appearance at school.

* Pack a kit for school emergencies. Stock it with personal items such as breath mints, pain relievers, and Band-Aids.

* Leave your desk and classroom neat at the end of the day. If you do, you will feel much better when you start the next day.

* If other teachers tell you off-putting or negative things about your students, ignore as much as you can. Ask them to tell you positive things instead.

* Anticipate and prepare for the stressful times in the school year: the beginning of the term, major holidays, exciting school events, standardized tests, and the end of the year.

* Learn your students' names as quickly as you can.

* Create an opening-of-class routine so that your students settle down quickly each day.

* Always have a backup plan.

* Remind yourself of other times when you have been successful and draw on those experiences.

1-12 Reflection: The Key to Becoming a Successful Educator

Even though teachers often informally mull over their successes and failures, wise teachers have learned that a systematic approach to reflection can play a key role in helping them grow professionally. To use reflection as a strategy for professional growth, try these suggestions:

* Make self-reflection a daily habit. For veteran teachers, setting aside time to consider the effectiveness of their teaching practices is an almost constant process.

* In order to reflect on your teaching practices in a beneficial way, you should formalize the system that you use for reflection.

    + Set aside time each day for reflection. Some teachers prefer to talk with colleagues; others find self-reflection helpful; and still others find that a combination of the two works best.

    + If you find that jotting notes is too time-consuming or cumbersome, consider using a small digital recorder to document your reflections.

    + If you save your reflections over a period of time, you will be able to see growth as well as refer to earlier insights and ideas.

        • As you try new activities or learn new skills, evaluate them as honestly as you can. Ask yourself questions such as these:

        • How can I improve the way I manage my disciplinary and academic responsibilities?

        • What lessons did I learn today?

        • What successes did I have today, and how did I achieve them?

CHAPTER 2

Learn to Work with Other Educators

2-1 Schools Require Teamwork

Because education is such an incredibly complex and worthy under-taking, teamwork is a crucial part of any school setting. Teachers need support from colleagues in order to have a positive impact on the lives of their students. When you become part of your school's team, here are just some of the benefits you will gain:

- Unified teachers can prevent misbehavior as well as combat other issues that adversely affect achievement.
- Guidance from your peers can increase your self-confidence.
- You will save time when you share ideas and responsibilities.
- When teachers share curriculum goals, they can focus their energy productively.
- It is personally satisfying to work with others for the greater good of the school.

Here are some useful suggestions on being the best team member you can be:

- Familiarize yourself with the goals that drive your school's improvement plan. What can you do to help achieve them?
- Be an active listener as you consider others' viewpoints.
- Learn to work well with all staff members, not just the faculty. Student success is everyone's responsibility.
- Maintain a good attendance record, and be on time to school and meetings.
- Be positive. Negativity makes any undertaking harder to accomplish.
- Be generous with your time, ideas, and materials.
- Be patient. When something goes wrong, don't assign blame.
- Be dependable. Honor your commitments, and be honest about your abilities, time constraints, and skills.
- Be proud of your school, and let that pride show.

- Be aware that everything you say and do affects your relationships with other teachers. Others should view you as capable, dedicated, and willing to learn.

- Make a point of learning about the culture and history of your school.

- Have high expectations for yourself as well as for your students. Others will respect you for this approach to your career.

- Base professional decisions on your commitment to successful student achievement.

- Ask for help when you need it. Veteran teachers don't expect you to know everything about teaching, but they do expect you to ask questions.

- Be quick to lend a helping hand. There are lots of jobs that a novice teacher can easily do. For example, volunteer to take notes at meetings.

- Everyone you work with has something to offer. Make an effort to learn as much as you can from other staff members.

- Remain open-minded. There are many different ways to accomplish the tasks that are required of you.

- Accept challenges. Project an enthusiastic, can-do attitude, and resist the urge to gripe on those days when you feel overwhelmed.

- Be respectful of the experience and expertise of your colleagues.

- Be careful not to reveal too much personal information. Not everyone in the teacher's lounge needs to know the details of your weekend adventures, for example.

- Be sure to give credit when it is due.

◆ Learn about the history and culture of your school. Use the Internet for research. Look at old yearbooks, and talk with people who have worked there for a while. When you show genuine interest in your school, you send the message that you appreciate the efforts of the educators who have gone before you.

◆ Participate in the life of the community where your students live, even if you do not live there. Attending community events, reading the local paper, and shopping in the area all indicate that you are willing to share in their experiences.

◆ Be courteous and friendly to everyone in your school, even when you are feeling stressed and overwhelmed.

◆ Eat lunch with other teachers. You need the break and the adult companionship.

◆ Stay a little late at the end of the day to work and visit with colleagues.

◆ Turn in all paperwork promptly. The office staff will appreciate your effort.

◆ Attend after-school events.

◆ Use school services. Check out books from the media center; take a wellness class, if one is offered; or occasionally visit the teachers' lounge, if your school has one.

◆ Make a point of learning the names of all staff members as quickly as you can.

◆ Pay attention at faculty meetings. Do not waste others' time during a meeting by asking questions that do not involve the entire group.

◆ Project an air of confidence and professionalism.

Successful communication means much more than just talking things over with peers. It's exchanging information in such a way that it can be easily understood. The guidelines that follow will help you develop these important skills.

General Guidelines

- It is respectful to address your coworkers by their title and last name in front of students.
- When you have to speak in front of a group, plan what you have to say so that you feel confident.
- Be sensitive to others' time restrictions. If you see that someone is busy, don't interrupt.
- Learn to pronounce and spell names correctly.

Written Communications and E-Mails

- Don't use your school's fax machine, supplies, or letterhead stationery for personal business.
- Don't use jargon when simpler language would be more appropriate.
- Before sending out a group mailing, check with a supervisor.
- The e-mails you send from school computers are subject to review by other school employees. Send e-mails at school for professional reasons only.
- Be aware that an e-mail can be forwarded to many other people with just a few clicks. Don't e-mail complaints or gossip.
- Respect the confidentiality of student information. Be careful how you identify students in e-mails.
- Readers will pay attention to your e-mails if they are concise, formatted well, and carefully edited.
- Before you write an e-mail, consider whether the message could be better conveyed by means of a quick phone call or a face-to-face conversation.

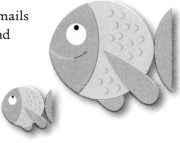

2-5   Professional Courtesy

Courtesy is the act of making the people around you feel comfortable. To accomplish this, you should learn as much as possible about the culture of your school and then adapt yourself to fit in. Follow these guidelines to make sure that all of your interactions with coworkers are as courteous as possible:

- Follow the Golden Rule: "Do unto others as you would have them do unto you."
- Pay attention to your personal grooming. Bad breath and unprofessional dress are both particularly noticeable in a school setting.
- Say "please" and "thank you."
- Pay attention when others are talking. Listen carefully to make sure you understand the discussion.
- If you are not feeling well, do your best not to infect others: wash your hands, cover your mouth when you cough, and stay home if you can.
- Respect others' personal space, and be careful not to borrow without permission.
- Be quick to publicly celebrate the success of others, and if you must criticize, do so privately.
- Pay attention in meetings. Don't multitask, leave early, or carry on a side conversation. Remember to turn off your cell phone.
- Be sensitive to others' feelings when discussing controversial topics such as politics, religion, or cultural issues.
- Keep the noise level in your classroom low enough that other classrooms are not affected.
- Introduce yourself when you meet someone new.
- Be nice to everyone you meet.

2-6 Suggestions for Working Well with Your Supervisors

You will have many interactions with your supervisors throughout the course of the school year; it only makes sense that you should work to ensure that the relationships you have with your supervisors are positive and professional. Learning to work well with the instructional leaders in your school will lead to a greater sense of confidence and satisfaction in your new career.

- Each of your supervisors has various responsibilities. Be sure to talk with the appropriate supervisor when you experience a problem. Always follow the chain of command.

- Behave in a professional manner at all times.

- Follow school rules, policies, and procedures.

- Pause before you criticize a supervisor. As a teacher, you know only a small part of the big picture at your school; you may not have a full understanding of a situation.

- Learn to take criticism gracefully.

- Be a little early to school, and stay a little late.

- Handle all but the most severe discipline problems yourself. Once you refer a child to the office, accept the decisions that the administrator makes about how to handle the situation.

- Check your paperwork; make sure that it is neat, accurate, and on time.

- Involve your supervisors in the successes in your classroom.

- Make sure that your relationships with parents and community members are constructive and professional.

- Keep your supervisors informed of positive and negative events in your classroom. Never allow a supervisor to be surprised by bad news.

- Don't make excuses.

- When you make a mistake, admit it. Never lie to a supervisor.

- When you need to speak with a supervisor, make an appointment.

- Be an active teacher who creates a classroom of active learners.

2-7 Guidelines to Help You Develop Productive Relationships with Mentors

Veteran as well as new teachers report that a positive relationship between mentor and mentee benefits both parties. Once you learn how to meet your day-to-day responsibilities, the conversation between you and your mentor can explore topics that result in shared professional growth.

- A worthwhile mentor-mentee relationship requires time and thoughtful effort from both participants in order to mature.

- The mentor and mentee should commit to working together in a businesslike manner.

- At the beginning of the year, your focus should be on such basics as school policies and procedures, how to obtain supplies, and how to get the year off to a good start.

- After you are settled into your school routine, the conversations you have with your mentor should be about how to set and achieve your goals for academics and for classroom management.

- Both parties in the relationship should be willing to share ideas, listen, learn, and grow.

- A sense of mutual trust is necessary for full collaboration. Both of you should handle sensitive issues in a discreet and diplomatic manner.

- A lack of common planning time is often an issue for mentors and their mentees. Consider as many different approaches as you can to deal with this problem. Sometimes a quick phone call or e-mail is all that is necessary.

- Successful meetings with a mentor require that you have a clear idea of your needs, that you are prepared, and that you stay focused on professional instead of personal concerns.

- One of your most important roles in a mentor-mentee relationship is to solicit constructive feedback on your teaching performance. Be open-minded when your mentor offers suggestions for improvement.

2-8   Work in Partnership with Substitute Teachers

Forming a successful partnership with substitute teachers creates a win-win situation for everyone involved; your sub will know what to do and your students will not lose valuable instruction time. To make this partnership work, put together a well-organized binder containing the following items:

- ☐ A phone number where you can be reached
- ☐ Class rolls with a pronunciation guide for student names
- ☐ A map of the school with exits and fire extinguishers marked
- ☐ Medical information for students with chronic illnesses such as asthma
- ☐ Your daily class and duty schedule
- ☐ A photo seating chart. Take a photo of each student, and attach it to a small self-sticking note. Stick the notes onto your chart, and slip the entire chart into a page protector.
- ☐ Class rules and consequences
- ☐ Classroom procedures for daily routines such as lunch and restroom requests as well as fire drills and other emergencies
- ☐ A list of several activities that students can do if they finish their assignments early
- ☐ Copies of all necessary forms such as lunch or attendance counts
- ☐ Names and room numbers of helpful teachers
- ☐ Lesson plans that are specifically written for the sub and not just copied from your plan book
  - ✦ Plan independent written work that will be collected and graded.
  - ✦ Photocopy, label, and organize all handouts. Don't leave busywork for students.
  - ✦ Avoid computer use, media center visits, and activities involving scissors or other sharp tools.

2-9 How to Deal with the Demands of Your Colleagues

Dealing with the demands of your colleagues requires a delicate balance of tact and enthusiasm as well as a large measure of common sense. Use these strategies to guide you as you learn to work well with all of your colleagues.

- When an administrator makes a reasonable request, you are expected to comply. You may be asked to take on after-school duties, sponsor student organizations, or even coach a team. If you are able to do this, you should comply with the request.

- Because administrators are your supervisors, you should make every effort to act in accordance with their rules and standards. For example, if your school district's dress code prohibits teachers from wearing caps in class and you choose to do so, then your refusal to follow the rule could be considered insubordinate.

- If a colleague asks you to take on an extra duty or task that makes you uncomfortable and that is an optional activity, politely decline.

- One way to forestall requests is to involve yourself in extra duties of your own choosing. Volunteer to sponsor a club that interests you, for example.

- A common area of dispute among colleagues is curriculum issues. If you are involved in a curriculum dispute, refer to your state guidelines. All instruction must satisfy those standards, even if you have colleagues who think differently.

- Try to be as open-minded, respectful, and tolerant as possible. Whenever you can pitch in or collaborate successfully, make it a point to do so.

2-10 Dealing with Difficult Colleagues

Because so much of a teacher's energy is devoted to cultivating professional relationships, it is not surprising that many teachers report conflicts with colleagues as a major cause of work-related stress. Use the following suggestions to deal with difficult coworkers and avoid the stress that can accompany conflicts with your colleagues:

- Be clear about your professional beliefs and responsibilities. This clarity will lend you confidence and make it harder for others to intimidate you.

- Avoid negative people, for negative attitudes spread quickly. Instead, associate with upbeat people who are focused on learning to be outstanding teachers.

- School can be extremely stressful at times. Don't be surprised to see normally serene coworkers lose their cool under pressure.

- If you find yourself in a conflict, try these suggestions for resolving it:

  + Instead of just reacting, respond by taking a problem-solving approach. Try to work out a resolution.

  + Instead of blaming the other person, think about how you may have contributed to the problem.

  + Refuse to act in kind if the other person has been rude or uncooperative.

  + Make sure that you are not overreacting or misreading the situation.

  + Talk privately but candidly with the other person. Ask, "What can we do to change this?"

  + Resist the urge to hash over the conflict with colleagues. Limit its negative impact by involving as few people as possible.

2-11 Join Other Educators in Online Learning Communities

You can connect with helpful local teachers as well as thousands of other educators by joining an online learning community in which you can share new ideas, lesson plans, support, and inspiration twenty-four hours a day.

The popularity of social networking sites such as Facebook (www.facebook.com) and MySpace (www.myspace.com) has made them ideal places to begin networking with other teachers. Explore some of the many forums and discussion groups offered by both of these sites as you connect with colleagues near and far.

In the following list, you will find a brief description of some of the other popular learning communities. All were free of charge at the time of publication.

- *A to Z Teacher Stuff (forums.atozteacherstuff.com).* On this site, you can interact with others in forums of interest to all teachers, especially new teachers.

- *TheApple (www.theapple.com).* Diverse groups, discussions, and forums make this one of the most popular sites for teachers on the Internet. You can join groups, participate in discussions, read and respond to blogs, and much more.

- *ProTeacher Community (www.proteacher.net).* Here you can find teacher chats, blogs, and discussions geared to teachers at many levels, from pre-kindergarten to eighth grade.

- *Teacher Focus (www.teacherfocus.com).* This site allows teachers to meet colleagues, chat, ask questions of experts, and browse thousands of articles posted by users.

- *Teacher Lingo (teacherlingo.com).* This blogging community connects readers with over one thousand bloggers at "Teacher Blogs."

- *Teachers Network (teachersnetwork.org).* The "New Teachers Helpline," staffed by experienced New York City teachers, guarantees a response to posted questions within seventy-two hours.

- *Teachers.Net (teachers.net).* This site offers over 150 teacher chat boards organized by grade level, curriculum, region, and special interests.

CHAPTER 3

Create a Link Between Home and School

3-1 Benefits of a Positive Relationship with Parents or Guardians

- Parents can share insights and past experiences that might help you understand and work productively with their child.

- Student stress will be reduced because parents and teachers work together to make sure students know how to manage their assignments.

- Parents will be less apt to schedule activities that conflict with important school events if they know about those events.

- Students do not keep testing boundaries because both teacher and parents are clear about what the boundaries are.

- Everyone wins when teachers and parents support each other's efforts to help a child.

- If students perceive that their parents like and accept you, then they will tend to be more accepting of you, too.

- Parents are less likely to believe falsehoods about how you manage your class or treat their child when you establish a relationship with them.

- When parents and teacher work together, student attendance tends to improve. When attendance improves, so does student achievement.

- Informed parents can provide help with activities such as fundraisers, donations, field trips, tutoring, and other class projects.

- If there is a problem at school, parents will be more willing to work with you because a sense of mutual trust and respect has already been established.

- A congenial and mutually supportive atmosphere sets a positive example of effective communication for students.

- You will be perceived as a caring educator by parents, colleagues, and your supervisors.

3-2 Questions You Should Ask Your Students' Parents

Because the responsibility of initiating a positive connection between school and home rests with you as the teacher and because it is important to learn as much as you can about your students, you should ask questions of the parents or guardians of your students. Use the following list of suggested questions to select the ones that are most appropriate for your students and your needs.

- What helpful hints can you give me about the best ways to teach your child?
- What obligations such as church activities, after-school jobs or classes, or family events does your child have?
- Are there any family situations that I should be aware of?
- What have you noticed about how your child learns best?
- What have your child's past school experiences been like?
- What is your child's attitude about school?
- How does your child respond to praise and rewards?
- What peer conflicts has your child had, and how were they resolved?
- How would you describe your child's optimum learning style?
- What behavior issues most concern you about your child?
- How would you describe your child's personality?
- What are your child's study habits like?
- How does your child manage homework assignments?
- How well does your child do when he or she works with other students in a group?
- What are your child's strengths as a student?
- What are your child's weaknesses as a student?

3-3 What Parents Expect of Their Child's Teacher

While not all parents or guardians will have the same expectations of their child's teacher, you can anticipate and plan for some similarities. Your students' parents will expect you to

- Ensure their child's safety while the child is in your class
- Be fair in your treatment of their child
- Recognize their child's unique gifts and talents
- Be reasonable in the amount of homework that you assign
- Follow school rules and policies
- Focus on positive qualities more than negative ones
- Contact them quickly if a problem arises
- Be courteous when you speak to their child
- Maintain an orderly classroom
- Be alert to the misbehavior of other students and how it may affect their child
- Look and act like a confident, skilled, professional educator
- Keep them apprised of scheduled events such as field trips and due dates for projects and tests
- Work with them for the benefit of their child
- Be able to meet with them before or after school
- Return phone calls promptly
- Be aware of any health issues that their child may have and act accordingly
- Protect their family's privacy
- Stay within the boundaries of your role as teacher
- Be honest with them
- Respect the confidentiality of their child's school records and progress reports
- Be willing to listen to them
- Talk to them before going to an administrator for help

3-4 Tips on Establishing Productive School-Home Relationships

- Teachers, not parents, should assume responsibility for communication. Be the first to reach out, and continue to keep the lines of communication open all year long.

- Keep the families of your students informed about classroom business through a combination of methods. Notes, Web pages, e-mail, phone calls, newsletters, and conferences are all good ways to keep in touch.

- Your students' parents or guardians will expect to be kept informed about topics such as these:

  - Class policies, rules, and consequences
  - Field trips and guest speakers
  - Homework and major assignments
  - Grading concerns
  - Reading lists
  - Positive things about their children
  - Tests and other assessments
  - Beginning-of-the-year information about necessary supplies, required texts, schedules, and other details

- Immediately call a parent or guardian if a child is hurt or ill.

- Make sure that parents or guardians know how to help their child be successful. Provide a syllabus, grade papers carefully, and be available to answer questions.

- Communicate early about problems. When you do, you are doing your part to keep the problem manageable and sending the message that you are cooperative.

- Comply with reasonable requests from parents whenever possible. Send home assignments when a child is ill, for example.

- Even if you develop a friendly relationship with a parent, you still must conduct yourself professionally; your first concern must be the child's welfare.

Phone Calls

- Lay the groundwork for a good relationship with parents and guardians by making positive phone calls during the first few days of school.
- When a parent leaves a message, return the call as soon as you can.
- When you call a parent, take time to prepare what you are going to say so that you can speak with confidence.
- Find a time and place to call in which you will not be interrupted.
- If you are calling about a problem, be sure to cool off before calling. Your anger will not solve the problem.
- When you call parents at work, begin by asking if they have time to talk. This courteous inquiry allows them to arrange for privacy.
- When calling a parent about a difficulty, always begin with a positive comment about their child and then calmly state your concern. Ask for the parent's support, and express your desire to work together with the parent.
- Listen carefully when parents speak. Take notes to ensure that you understand their concerns and that you both share the same point of view about the problem.
- Document the conversation.

Notes and E-Mails

- Take a businesslike and friendly tone. Use a respectful greeting and closing.
- Don't go into great detail if there is a problem. Make a phone call instead.
- Write neatly, or type. Proofread carefully.
- If you are sending a message with a student, unobtrusively place the note in an envelope for the child to take home. Ask that the message be signed and returned.

3-6   Strategies for Managing Formal Parent Conferences Successfully

- Although you may feel intimidated at the thought of a formal conference, remember that parents and students also feel anxious.

- Be clear about the purpose of the conference when you schedule it. Do you need to solve a problem or just discuss information?

- Make notes on what you need to say, and gather the papers you will need to make your points.

- Review grades and other records in order to be fully prepared.

- Arrange for a translator, if necessary.

- Be sure to arrange your schedule so that you can meet without interruption.

- Set up the conference area with the guest's comfort in mind. Provide a table and chairs rather than student desks, if possible.

- Always allow parents to talk first, especially if they are there to settle a problem and not just gather information.

- Listen attentively. Take notes, if necessary.

- Speak only after parents have finished. Then, be specific about your concerns and convey your willingness to work with them for the welfare of their child.

- Be careful to detail the steps you have already taken to solve any problems.

- Work together with parents to develop a solution you can all agree on.

- End with a restatement of what each party has agreed to do, and express your appreciation for the time they have spent.

- After the meeting, go over your notes and document the meeting in your parent contact log.

3-7 How to Handle Conflicts with Parents or Guardians

- Set the table for success in conflict resolution early in the year by developing positive relationships with the parents or guardians of your students. You can avoid many conflicts if you spend time developing a good working relationship early.

- Strive to prevent or minimize conflicts by following these suggestions:

  - Create strong relationships with students.
  - Follow school rules, policies, and procedures.
  - Use common sense.
  - Contact parents about problems while problems are still small.
  - Keep documentation about problems up to date.

- When there is a conflict, remember that your purpose is not to voice negative emotions but rather to solve the problem.

- In a confrontation, allow parents to speak first . Listen quietly until they finish saying what they need to say. Only then should you present your point of view.

- Calmly and respectfully state your point of view. Be factual, precise, and tactful.

- Make it clear to parents that you want what's best for their child. Be as flexible, accommodating, and open-minded as you can be.

- Don't lose your temper. You will accomplish nothing except appearing unprofessional.

- Document the contact, being careful to give a detailed account that you can refer to later.

- Do not allow parents to be abusive. Contact an administrator for help.

- If you believe that the issue is not resolved, inform an administrator before the angry parents do.

3-8 Courteous Interactions with Non-Nuclear Families

- Although it may seem a small issue to a busy teacher, being concerned enough to learn about the familial relationships of your students is necessary for successful interactions with them. You should know who the significant adults in their lives are and how those adults are related to your students.

- Be aware of wording that may be casually insensitive or hurtful to students who do not live in a nuclear home. For example, telling your class, "Have your mom sign this" when sending home a paper may be hurtful to students who do not live with their mothers. Instead, try "Take this home to be signed."

- Avoid addressing general notes and correspondence only to parents. Try "parents or guardians" instead.

- When you set up a contact information file for each student, make note of the correct titles and names of parents or guardians so that you can address them respectfully.

- Be aware of which family member you should address when you have concerns about a particular student. If you have to call a student's home, don't relay unpleasant news to the first person who answers the phone. Wait to speak to the child's parent or guardian.

- Don't assume that the parents or guardians of a student are not fully involved in the child's life just because the child is not a member of a nuclear family.

Many teachers find that it is easier to keep up with paperwork related to student information if they create a file for each student. In that way, much of the paperwork related to each child can be stored in one place.

- *Contact information:* Have students or their parents fill out an information form with e-mail and mailing addresses as well as phone numbers. Make a copy of the completed form. Store the original in the student's folder, and put the copies in alphabetical order in a binder to use at home.

- *Medical information:* File all information in the student's folder.

- *Behavior information:* Create and print a page for each child with space to list any offenses, the date they occurred, interventions, and notes. File this page in the child's folder, along with copies of referral and other notices.

- *Attendance information:* Store all notes from home in the student's file. Be sure to either print and store or save relevant e-mails. Attendance records must be meticulously accurate and kept on file all year.

Contact with parents should be documented. Use a binder to store this information. Create and print a page for each child with space for the name of the person you spoke to, the date, time, reason, type of contact, and outcome. Record each contact promptly.

504 plans and IEP information are confidential and must be kept in a secure area.

Grades are confidential information. Do not post them or share them with an unauthorized person. Follow your district's protocols for keeping grades secure.

Section Two

Create a Positive Class Culture

A positive class culture is a vital component of successful teaching. When students and teachers work together in a productive, cooperative environment, the synergy of that positive culture transcends daily concerns and allows a focus on student achievement and success.

IN CHAPTER FOUR, you will learn how to set up your classroom so that students will feel comfortable and able to work together in safe, child-centered, well-organized surroundings.

IN CHAPTER FIVE, you will learn how to connect with each of your students in order to build the kind of inspiring relationship that is mutually beneficial to students and teachers. From practical tips to help you be a better teacher for students who are struggling to suggestions on how to relate well to every child in your care, the ideas in this chapter will help you define your role in this relationship.

IN CHAPTER SIX, you will discover principles and strategies of motivation that will make it easier for you to engage your students in meaningful, relevant work all year long. You'll examine the role of extrinsic and intrinsic motivation techniques in making every child into a capable, confident learner.

IN CHAPTER SEVEN, you will examine some of the powerful tools that can help you prevent misbehavior. You'll learn some of the reasons that students misbehave, how to set class rules and procedures, and simple strategies to prevent cheating.

IN CHAPTER EIGHT, you will learn what to do once a student misbehaves so that the rest of your class is not affected in a negative way. You'll learn when and how to effectively handle misbehaviors yourself, when you should call a parent or involve an administrator, and how to respond to student violence.

CHAPTER 4

Make Your Classroom a Productive Learning Environment

4-1 The Essentials of a Productive Learning Environment

A productive learning environment will serve these purposes:

- Make it easier for you to teach and for students to learn
- Welcome students so that they feel valued and appreciated
- Encourage student achievement and effort
- Provide a safe place for students

To create a well-ordered classroom that is a pleasant work space, consider adapting the following suggestions:

- Be careful to consider traffic flow patterns when planning room arrangements so that students can move about with ease.
- Equip your room with furniture and materials that are comfortable, age-appropriate, and practical.
- Create flexible arrangements of furniture and materials that take into account the various tasks that must be performed in your classroom each day.
- Make sure that the furniture is the correct size for your students. Each child should have a comfortable place to work.
- Position furniture so that students are able to see the instructor during whole-group instruction and the instructor is able to see all students at all times.
- Encourage student independence and ownership of their learning with readily accessible materials that students can locate and distribute themselves.
- Make every effort to provide a space with adequate lighting and a comfortable temperature.
- Aim for some decorations that directly instruct students and some that indirectly instruct them. For example, a word wall provides direct instruction and a wall of photographs of your students working together provides indirect instruction and encouragement.

4-2 The First Step: Evaluate the Room

⚙ You will save time if you take a digital camera, paper, a pencil, and a tape measure with you on your first visit to your classroom. Photograph the room thoroughly, and be sure to measure areas such as shelves, storage areas, bulletin boards, and the chalkboard or whiteboard.

⚙ Be on the lookout for equipment and furniture that need repair or that pose safety concerns. Make note of any necessary repairs.

⚙ Survey the room for items or areas that have the potential to distract your students.

⚙ Count the student desks, tables, chairs, and computers to determine whether you have enough of each for your students.

⚙ Survey the room to determine whether you have these other essential classroom items:

- ❑ Keys to the door and any lockable cabinets
- ❑ Operating instructions for the heating and cooling systems
- ❑ Windows and blinds that are clean and in good repair
- ❑ Sufficient lighting
- ❑ Overhead projector and screen
- ❑ Bookshelves
- ❑ A desk and chair for the teacher
- ❑ Empty and usable file cabinets
- ❑ At least one pencil sharpener
- ❑ At least one trash container
- ❑ A computer for the teacher to use
- ❑ A classroom phone
- ❑ An intercom system
- ❑ An American flag on display
- ❑ A television monitor
- ❑ A clock

4-3 Create a Safe Classroom

When you plan the productive learning environment that you want for your students, the most important aspect should be safety. To make sure your classroom is safe, try these suggestions:

- Never leave students unsupervised.

- Learn your school's procedures for emergencies such as fire drills, tornado drills, or protocols for intruders in the building.

- Be aware of the procedures you will need to follow to assist your students who have chronic illnesses.

- Secure all electrical cords so that students do not harm themselves. Check to make sure that the outlets are also operating correctly, too.

- Check the windows to make sure the panes and screens are in good working condition.

- Keep your classroom as sanitary as possible. Epidemics such as the recent staph outbreak make this precaution more important than ever.

- Don't leave your classroom unlocked when you are not present.

- Stabilize all bookcases and other tall pieces of equipment so that they can't tip over. Make sure all objects on them are also placed securely.

- Establish a lockable area in your room for your personal belongings and for confidential documents.

- All sharp objects such as scissors should be stored out of sight until you are ready to issue them.

- Make sure the cleaning supplies you use are not harmful to your students. Read the labels carefully, and check your school district's policy about acceptable cleaning supplies.

- Make it easy for students to move about. Space desks carefully, and don't block the exits to your classroom.

4-4 Arrange Your Classroom for Learning

- Begin your room arrangement with large items of furniture such as bookcases and file cabinets because their placement will probably be permanent.

- Put bookcases and other large objects against a wall.

- Student desks should be in the middle and front of the room.

- Try to spread students out as much as you can. If your classroom is overcrowded, arrange desks in rows to maximize space.

- You will need an area where you can confer with students in small groups.

- Consider traffic flow. What routes will students have to take to sharpen pencils, staple and turn in papers, dispose of trash, and pick up materials?

- The teacher's desk should be in the back of the room so that you can observe all students as they work without disturbing them.

- Save time and steps by placing a file cabinet, bookcase, and computer near your desk.

- You will need to set up an instructional area in the front of the room where you can deliver information, give directions, or demonstrate an activity. You will probably need a chair, stool, lectern, or table for this purpose.

- Using two trash cans will minimize distractions caused by students walking around in search of the container as well as make it easier to keep the room neat.

- Supplies need to be neatly stored in a logical and orderly fashion so that your students won't waste instruction time locating them.

- Minimize distractions with careful placement of furniture or equipment. For example, do not place student desks near an open door.

4-5   Create Effective Seating Arrangements

Even though it takes time to create an effective seating arrangement, your effort will be rewarded with increased student engagement and decreased misbehavior. Try the following suggestions to optimize the seating arrangements in your class.

- Remember these simple keys to successful seating arrangements: all students can see and hear you; you can see everyone; and the focus is on instruction and not on distractions.

- Attend to the needs of all your students when assigning them a seat. Some students may require preferential seating—for example, to accommodate a visual or hearing impairment. Still other students may have different special accommodations such as being seated in an area where a special education teacher can help them unobtrusively.

- Many teachers have found that a U-shaped arrangement, with a smaller U of desks inside a larger one, works well for them. This arrangement enables students to see the instructor and their classmates at the same time.

- At the start of the year, consider using traditional rows, to allow students to focus on you as you teach procedures, rules, and expectations.

- Once you are comfortable with the behavior of your students, arrange desks so that they can be moved into groups quickly and easily.

- Some classrooms such as laboratories, music classrooms, and art classrooms pose challenges because they are primarily set up as work areas. Handle these challenges by teaching procedures that encourage students to focus on the teacher instead of classmates.

- Don't seat easily sidetracked students near windows, pencil sharpeners, or other distracting areas.

- If you want to promote class discussion, have students sit in a circle.

4-6 How to Organize Your Own Work Area

Organizing your work area is a challenging task because you must create a private space within a very public area.

- Arrange your work area efficiently in a triangle with your desk, filing cabinets, and book shelves as the points.

- Teach students not to take items from your desk without your permission.

- Your desktop should reflect your personality but also be businesslike and professional.

- Many teachers find it easy to stay organized by developing colored-coded systems for managing various types of papers.

- You will also need to create systems for organizing electronic paperwork such as e-mail, grades, software programs, and passwords.

- Save time by labeling everything with large, easy-to-read letters. Be specific. For example, a folder labeled "Plans" is not as helpful as one labeled with the name of a particular unit of study.

- Organize desk drawers by grouping similar things together. Keep the things you use frequently near the front and the materials you use less frequently at the back of each drawer.

- Many teachers prefer three-ring binders to keep papers organized. Be sure to color-code and label the spines for quick reference.

- You will need a calendar, a to-do list, and a place to record appointments, messages, and other important information.

- If you leave your desk clean at the end of the day, you will find that the start of the next day will be more pleasant and productive.

4-7 Make Your Classroom Greener by Using Paper Wisely

⚙ Increase your students' understanding of the importance of an environmentally friendly classroom by making them aware of the thousands of tons of school paper waste that go to landfills every year.

⚙ If your school does not already have a recycling program, consider starting one. Contact your local municipality offices for more information.

⚙ Use both sides of a sheet of paper. Carefully plan your handouts, and allow students to write on the backs of their own papers.

⚙ Proofread and use the preview feature on your computer before printing to avoid wasting paper by having to reprint.

⚙ Use a projector in place of handouts whenever it's practical to do so.

⚙ Encourage students to practice on the board. Individual white-boards can also be reused with just a swipe of an old sock.

⚙ Allow students to e-mail you their homework whenever possible.

⚙ Set aside an area where students who have written on only one side of a sheet can store old papers and reuse them. You can also save old memos, flyers, posters, and other one-sided papers for students to use again.

⚙ If a sheet has a wide margin, have students cut the excess into note cards and use them for short notes.

⚙ Use rags for cleaning cloths instead of paper towels.

⚙ Purchase recycled paper products whenever you can.

Basic Teaching Supplies

- Personal planner or calendar
- An easy-to-find key ring for room and cabinet keys
- Three-ring binders
- Notebook paper
- Notepads
- Pens
- Pencils
- Highlighters
- Self-sticking notes
- Staplers
- Staples
- Hole punch
- File folders
- Labels
- Scissors
- Stackable trays
- Calculator
- Transparent tape
- Masking tape
- Rubber bands
- Paper clips
- Correction fluid
- Stickers
- Note cards
- Stationery for thank-you notes
- Rulers
- Safety pins
- Colored pencils
- Crayons
- Glue
- Construction paper
- Storage bins
- Adhesive bandages
- Tissues
- Chalk
- Board markers
- Board erasers
- Overhead transparencies
- Overhead pens
- Computer memory storage devices

Basic Professional Documents

- Faculty handbook
- Curriculum guides
- Lesson plan book
- Grade book
- Professional portfolio
- Information on emergency procedures
- Student contact information
- Staff contact information

4-9   Create a Student-Centered Environment

Your classroom should be welcoming and student-centered. Each student should feel that he or she contributes to the success of everyone in the room. This type of environment will reward your efforts in several ways:

- A focus on instruction that increases student achievement
- A bond among students and between teacher and pupils
- Reduced misbehavior
- A sense of pride and school spirit

There are many ways to create a student-centered environment:

- Display photos of your students engaged in various activities.
- Post newspaper articles that feature your students.
- Have a recognition area that showcases students' achievements as individuals or as a class.
- Pay attention to students' comfort. Your room should be furnished with user-friendly equipment, spaces for various activities, a comfortable chair or rug, and other articles that will add to their sense of well-being.
- Hang encouraging mottoes and posters.
- Use attractive colors that appeal to your students. Inquire about what colors they would like to see in their classroom.
- Set a shared class goal, and graph the progress your students make toward achieving that goal.
- Create a bank of shared supplies for students who may need to borrow paper or pencils.
- Post a question, puzzle, or brainteaser of the day for students to enjoy.
- Encourage student ownership of some interactive parts of the room such as word walls, calendars, or message boards.

Background Materials

- Old maps
- Newspapers
- Magazine pages and covers
- Brochures
- Brown paper
- Phone book pages
- Enlarged clip art
- Student artwork
- Photos printed on colorful paper
- Pages from discarded books
- Jigsaw puzzle pieces
- Postcards
- Greeting cards
- Felt
- Burlap
- Wallpaper
- Curtains from a thrift store
- Inexpensive fabric
- Calendar photos
- Student photos
- Wrapping paper
- School spirit items
- Book jackets
- Coloring book pages

Three-Dimensional Effects

- Styrofoam
- Lightweight objects or figurines
- Cotton balls
- Leaves and branches
- Party items
- Pipe cleaners

Borders

- Ticket stubs
- Fringe
- Crepe paper
- Wallpaper borders
- Play money
- Garlands and tinsel
- Bookmarks

Note: If the materials you use are not flame-retardant, use a flame-retardant spray to make them safe for your classroom.

4-11 Don't Just Decorate, Instruct!

Although your classroom decor should be attractive, the emphasis should be on creating an environment that teaches content. Here are some ways that you can use the decor of your classroom as a teaching tool:

- Post a daily word, fact, Web site, open-ended question, study skill, brainteaser, current event, or problem.

- Display photos, models, posters, articles, various types of maps, primary source documents, or other items related to the content under study.

- Display advice from various experts, older students, or well-known people on how to succeed academically.

- Set aside areas of your room in which students can work independently on reading, writing, board games, practice items, or remediation or enrichment materials.

- Use word walls to create an interactive representation of the key vocabulary terms in a unit of study. Here's how:

  + Display the words you want to use on typed or handwritten note cards, on cutout images or shapes, on chalkboards, or on dry erase boards.

  + Although they were originally used in classrooms for younger students, word walls can be used in almost any classroom to

    - Introduce new words

    - Arouse interest in an upcoming unit of study

    - Reinforce learning and vocabulary acquisition

    - Help students make the connection between new learning and previous knowledge

  + Introduce no more than ten words a week. As students master the words, remove them and add others. The ones you remove can be used for review.

4-12 Display Student Work

When you display student work, you make it clear that you appreciate your students and their efforts, generate enormous pride, and encourage hard work. This practice also allows students to share good ideas and learn from each other.

- Display photos of students that show them working or holding their work.

- Be inclusive with the work that you display. All students should see their work presented.

- Before you display work, ask students for permission.

- Never display graded work or papers with errors you've marked. If you need to grade the work, tell students privately what grades they earned.

- Show that you respect students' efforts by taking good care of student work. Mount it carefully.

- Be sure to make the display more meaningful for your class by involving students as you plan how to show their work.

- Here are some easy ways to display student work:

  - Hang work from the ceiling, clip it to window blinds, put it on cabinet doors, or use project display boards or unused spaces as exhibit areas.

  - Have students make their own books or scrapbooks.

  - For younger students, assign a permanent place for each child to display his or her work, if space allows.

- Work does not have to be displayed just within the four walls of your classroom. Instead, show it at your school office or media center, at local businesses, or at public libraries. You can even post it online (if you have parental permission).

CHAPTER 5

Forge Positive Relationships with Students

5-1 Characteristics of an Appropriate Teacher-Student Relationship

While no one wants to be accused of misconduct, it is a fact that all teachers are vulnerable to allegations of improper relationships with students. To avoid such allegations and to become an effective teacher instead, let the characteristics in the following lists guide your interactions with students.

In an inappropriate relationship, the teacher

- Assumes a parental role
- Shares too much intimate information
- Becomes hostile to certain students
- Is alone with students
- Loses sight of the immaturity of the child
- Socializes with students
- Allows students to invade personal space
- Tries to be the students' friend

In an appropriate relationship, the teacher

- Serves as a friendly adult whose primary concern is a child's best interests
- Guides students as they learn to make good choices
- Protects students from harm
- Is familiar with students' social, academic, and behavioral circumstances
- Helps students develop insights into the world around them
- Provides opportunities and encouragement as students work to achieve goals
- Shows affection and acceptance
- Is the students' advocate
- Makes students aware of their strengths and helps them correct weaknesses
- Is able to say no in a firm and pleasant way
- Treats students with respectful courtesy and expects to be treated likewise
- Empowers students by having high expectations for their success

5-2   What Students Expect of You

Just as you have expectations for the academic and behavioral performance of your students, they have expectations of you. Although students' expectations will vary, depending on factors such as their age and ability level, certain student expectations appear to be universal. Your students will expect you to

- Enjoy being with them
- Appreciate them for who they are
- Set a positive, supportive tone for the class
- Show that you enjoy the classes that you teach
- Know the subject matter that you are teaching
- Help them make good grades
- Keep them busy with meaningful work
- Protect them from bullies
- Be fair in the way that you treat all students
- Have a sense of humor
- Help them prepare for and pass standardized tests
- Show that you have self-control
- Ask about their life outside of school
- Be very organized and neat
- Make their classroom child-friendly
- Enforce class rules
- Be happy for them when they are successful
- Be prepared for class
- Not assign too much homework
- Listen to them when a problem arises
- Prevent disruptive students from ruling the classroom
- Reward effort as well as achievement
- Remember what it was like to be their age

5-3 The Greatest Gift: High Expectations

Paradoxical as it may seem, holding high expectations for the academic and behavioral performance of all students is perhaps the greatest gift that teachers can offer. Students will rise to meet even the most challenging expectations if you offer nurturing support and guidance.

- Tell students that you do not intend to give up until they are successful in your class.

- Focus on your students' strong points. Too often, teachers focus on correcting weaknesses instead of encouraging students to take advantage of their strengths.

- Place students in mixed-ability groups. When teachers group low achievers separately, it sends a message of defeat.

- Offer a mixture of assessment types so that students can demonstrate their knowledge in a variety of ways.

- Instill a sense of responsibility for their own success in your students. Having students work toward a personal goal is an excellent way to do this.

- Display encouraging mottoes and slogans from achievers who struggled early in life.

- Provide ongoing support for less-proficient learners as well as enrichment opportunities for all students.

- Build intrinsic motivation into every lesson. Offer small tangible rewards occasionally, too.

- Have students share successful study strategies with classmates. Informal peer support can be a powerful tool.

- While you should never water down the curriculum, you should alter the way you teach it so that all students can learn.

- With older students, take time to discuss the dangers of substance abuse, gangs, and unprotected sex.

5-4 Tips to Help You Gather Information About Your Students

* Speak with the child's previous teachers, being careful to elicit a balanced, professional response, not an emotional reaction.

* Carefully study your students' permanent records.

* Observe your students as they work, to look for specific information such as relationships among classmates, how they approach a test, or what causes off-task behavior.

* Pay attention to students' body language. Many emotions are telegraphed unconsciously through body language.

* Talk with students' parents and family members. Ask them to fill out questionnaires or write brief notes about their child.

* Administer inventories to assess students' learning styles.

* Ask students to write personal responses to various topics through journals, exit slips, or learning logs.

* Notice how students relate to each other in casual settings and during group work.

* Study the work products that your students create, to learn what interests them and where their talents lie.

* Have students complete interest inventories.

* Pay attention to the books that your students read and to the television shows, games, and music that interest them.

* Talk with students about how they prefer to organize their personal belongings and class work.

* Ask students to describe themselves. You can ask for this in writing or during personal conferences.

* Offer students icebreakers and team-building exercises, and pay attention to their interactions.

5-5 Respect Your Students' Dignity

Because of the delicate nature of relationships between teachers and their students, it is important that you use your adult power to show respect to your students. This attitude will yield countless rewards for a long time. You treat students with respect when you take these actions:

- Expect academic and behavioral success of all students.
- Avoid backing students into corners; always allow them a way to avoid embarrassment.
- Acknowledge complaints and allow students to voice their concerns.
- Teach citizenship and social skills as part of the daily fabric of your class. Such lessons don't have to be time-consuming to be effective.
- Use time-outs and other interventions that can help students compose themselves during a conflict.
- Provide predictable routines and procedures so that students can go about their work, confident that they know what to do.
- Avoid power struggles, especially in front of other students.
- Don't comment on a child's appearance.
- Never threaten or scold a student in front of other students.
- Don't call attention to a child's status or family situation.
- Never insult a student in jest or allow others to do the same.
- Make courteous behavior the norm in your class.
- Don't allow students to grade each other's work.
- Arrange a private signal with impulsive students that you can use to help them redirect themselves.
- Offer constructive feedback on papers instead of just marking errors.
- Encourage, encourage, encourage.

5-6 Strategies to Help Students Who Are Reluctant Learners

- Strive to determine the causes of the child's reluctance. Too often, teachers just view a student as lazy or react in anger instead of taking a problem-solving approach.
- Strengthen basic skills in reading, writing, and math.
- Make sure that students know the purpose for their work by teaching them to be goal-oriented. Set both long-term and short-term goals together.
- Try not to overwhelm the reluctant student with a large amount of practice work.
- Teach students efficient shortcuts that take the tedium out of assignments.
- Offer instruction that appeals to various learning styles.
- If you notice that students are not working, ask them to tell you what they already know. Often, this will encourage them to continue.
- Offer help to students who feel that their work must be perfect before they turn it in.
- Establish a strong personal connection with reluctant learners.
- Show that you value students' contributions to the class and that they are missed when absent.
- Stress the practical value of what students are learning.
- Provide an authentic audience as often as possible. For example, a report on how to improve a city's water quality addressed to a local government official is more interesting for students than one written for only a teacher to read.
- Build students' confidence. Students who feel capable will try harder than those who don't.
- Stress the relationship between effort and outcome.
- Appeal to students' interests and sense of fun in order to help motivate them.
- Involve students in authentic, cooperative projects that offer help to others who are less fortunate.
- Involve students in work that requires cooperative learning, technology, inquiry, critical thinking, or responding to open-ended questions.

5-7 Strategies to Help Students with Special Needs

Although students may have many different types of special needs, several strategies can transcend these differences and allow you to connect with your special needs students. Use the strategies in the following list to help your special needs students reach their fullest potential.

* You do not want to embarrass students. Respect the confidentiality of student information. Be careful with paperwork and discreet in what you say.

* Make your classroom as comfortable and inviting as possible by making sure that students with disabilities can move around easily, access materials, and have decorations that engage their interest.

* Lessen distraction through careful furniture placement and reduction of visual distractions.

* Allow students to take frequent, structured breaks. Use a timer or other signal to manage breaks.

* Use carefully selected audiotapes, art, and other media to make instruction accessible and interesting.

* Be ready to provide materials and supplies for students who come to class unprepared.

* Provide alternative ways for a child to complete an assignment—for example, by providing answers on a voice recorder or using a calculator.

* Allow students to retake a test after remediation.

* Use frequent rewards for effort as well as achievement.

* Establish clear rules and consequences.

* Segment work into smaller, manageable sections so that students are not overwhelmed.

* Learn from the support personnel and the parents of your special needs students.

* Use plenty of models, demonstrations, and examples to clarify instruction.

* Be positive by focusing on students' achievements instead of their weaknesses as you work to build their confidence.

5-8 Strategies to Help Students with Attention Disorders

Try the strategies in the following list to help students in your class who have attention disorders such as attention deficit disorder (ADD) or attention-deficit/hyperactivity disorder (AD/HD) to channel their energy and curb their impulsivity.

- Shorten tests and practice work so you don't overwhelm students with attention disorders.

- Have students practice estimating how long it will take to complete an assignment so that they can remain focused within that time limit.

- Use various media to capture and hold students' attention.

- Seat students with attention disorders in a quiet place with as few distractions as possible.

- Help students with attention disorders stay on track while reading by holding a note card or strip of paper under the line that is being read and moving it down the page as the text is read.

- Some students with attention deficits find it easier to comprehend material if they read it along with an audio recording.

- Break instructions into small steps, and repeat them as needed. Refer to a written copy, when possible.

- Provide outlines or notes for lectures or long reading assignments.

- Set up a system for students to record homework assignments once they are given so that they can plan their work.

- Teach organization strategies for maintaining materials. For example, teach students to pack their book bags at night.

- Provide syllabi, daily checklists, and other reminders, to help students plan ahead.

- Review material several times a day in short, frequent bursts.

- Many students with attention disorders find it easier to type than to write by hand and should be allowed to do so, if possible.

- Keep the materials required for your class to a minimum so that students will not have trouble keeping up with them.

Part of building the successful relationship that you want to have with your students involves a commitment to teaching good citizenship. Focus first on the traits of good citizenship that you would like to promote in your class, and then create activities to strengthen those traits.

* These traits are ones that all teachers can encourage:
  + Compassion
  + Generosity
  + Respect
  + Tolerance
  + Responsibility
  + Fairness
  + Integrity
  + Courtesy

* Activities that will make the traits of good citizens part of your classroom will vary according to the age and sophistication of your students.
  + Be on the lookout for good behavior, and when you see it, label it as a positive trait so that students can see that it is part of a larger pattern of citizenship.
  + Have students write thank-you notes to school and community members and make a habit of thanking each other for small kindnesses.
  + Have your students keep track of the acts of kindness they perform each week.
  + Model the behavior you want. Let students see you pick up trash, recycle paper, or show appreciation.
  + Stop occasionally to explain which trait is connected to an action you take.
  + Choose a positive trait each week as a focus. Put a mark on the board every time you notice it in your class, and you will reinforce that trait.
  + Ask your students to tell you how they are already good citizens and how they could be better ones.

- Let your expression reflect the pleasure that you take in your students' presence.

- Have no invisible students in your class. Speak every child's name every day.

- Find the positive aspects of a student's character, and emphasize them.

- Contact a child's home with good news.

- Put stickers on student papers.

- Write personal notes to students.

- Acknowledge it when a student is having a bad day, and offer to help if you can.

- Ask about an event that a child is anticipating.

- Celebrate birthdays and other special occasions.

- Attend after-school games, performances, and activities.

- When a child speaks to you, stop what you are doing and really listen.

- Assign the work groups in your class. Don't let cliques choose their friends.

- Schedule team-building activities when you place students in groups so they can learn to work well together.

- Set class goals, and work together as a team to achieve them.

- Let your voice be the kindest one your students hear all day.

- If a child is ill, pay attention. Send him or her to the nurse. Call his or her parents or guardian. Be sympathetic.

- Call on all of your students, not just the ones who you think might know the answer.

- Design activities that place value on students helping each other succeed. A flash card review is a good example of this type of activity.

CHAPTER 6

Create Opportunities for Student Success

6-1   The Principles of Motivation

- *All learning must have a purpose.* Teachers and students should work together to establish long-term goals so that class work is relevant to students' lives and driven by a purpose.

- *Students need the skills and knowledge necessary to complete their work and achieve their goals.* Help students achieve short-term goals in order to develop the competencies they need to be successful.

- *Specific directions empower students.* When students know exactly what they must do to complete assignments, they will approach their work with confidence and interest.

- *Students want to have fun while they work.* Teachers who offer enjoyable learning activities find that students are less likely to be off task.

- *Offer activities that involve higher-order thinking skills.* Students find open-ended questions and critical thinking more engaging than activities that just involve recalling facts.

- *Curiosity is an important component of motivation.* When students want to learn more about a topic, they will tackle challenging assignments in order to satisfy their curiosity.

- *A blend of praise and encouragement is effective in building self-reliance.* Teachers who offer sincere praise and encouragement establish a positive, nurturing classroom atmosphere.

- *A combination of extrinsic and intrinsic rewards increases student focus and on-task behavior.* When used separately, both types of rewards motivate students. However, when teachers combine them, the effect is much greater.

- *Involve students in collaborative activities.* When students work together, both motivation and achievement soar.

6-2 Positive Teacher Attitudes That Create Student Success

- Because students will rise to their teachers' expectations, it is crucial that those expectations be high.

- All students should be absolutely certain that their teachers like and respect them.

- Teachers who focus on the times when their students are correct instead of just on the mistakes they make will create students who work hard to be correct as often as possible.

- Teachers who believe that their students are capable learners will have students who become capable learners.

- It is vital that all students feel included in all class activities.

- Making students part of a team approach to learning will involve them more deeply than if their work is defined totally by a teacher.

- It is important for teachers to listen carefully to their students.

- Students need to hear their teachers say pleasant, encouraging things to them in order to become self-directed.

- Teachers must think before they act if they want to help students make wise choices for themselves.

- The unexpected will happen every day at school. Plan for it.

- Enlarging a student's world through reading, new experiences, and technology sets the stage for future learning.

- Students need to have their effort made visible through displays of their work and positive written feedback.

- It is more important to push students toward self-discipline than to be the controller of behavior in a classroom.

- Class activities should be fun as well as educational.

6-3 Questions to Help You Provide Opportunities for Success

- How can I convey my belief in my students' ability to learn successfully?

- How can I help students set goals and work to achieve them?

- How can I design instruction that allows students to build on their previous success?

- How can I design instruction that allows students to connect their learning to previous knowledge?

- How can I build my students' confidence in their ability to master the material successfully?

- How can I challenge students without causing them stress?

- How can I help students see the big picture of what they need to learn so that they can understand the reasons for the various assignments they have to do?

- How can I help my students learn to track their own progress and use self-evaluation to determine their own skill and knowledge levels?

- How can I reward successful students in such a way that all students will want to be successful?

- How can I teach my students the study skills they will need to accomplish their work?

- How can I teach content so that students will want to acquire essential understanding?

- How can I provide opportunities for students to assess their strengths and weaknesses as learners?

- How can I remediate and enrich instruction so that all students reach success?

- How can I motivate students to keep trying even when the work is challenging?

6-4 Questions to Help You Provide Opportunities for Enjoyment

- How can I offer my students options so that they can choose activities that they enjoy?
- How can I include activities with wow factors?
- How can I convey my own enthusiasm for the material under study?
- How can I break up class routines by adding occasional novelty?
- How can I create a sense of suspense that will intrigue and engage students?
- How can I include hands-on activities that energize the learning climate?
- How can I use open-ended questions to keep students engaged?
- How can I make sure my students have fun and learn at the same time?
- How can I design instruction so that my students are active partners in the learning process?
- How can I help students recap a lesson and review material through activities that are interesting and productive at the same time?
- How can I incorporate technology resources that will interest my students?
- How can I offer instruction based on critical thinking skills that require students to think differently about a topic?
- How can I make seatwork enjoyable?
- How can I offer enjoyable multimedia resources that will enable my students to learn and have fun at the same time?
- How can I learn more about the kinds of activities that my students would enjoy?
- How can I make sure to cover objectives while providing activities that my students will enjoy?

6-5 Questions to Help You Provide Opportunities for Students to Feel a Sense of Belonging

- How can I make sure that every student feels welcomed in my classroom?

- How can I create effective work groups so that students work together productively?

- How can I provide support for individual students so that they have the social skills necessary to fit in at school?

- How can I provide support for groups so that they work together in an effective way?

- How can I help students create study groups?

- How can I make it easy for students to learn about each other's strengths so that they can work well together?

- How can I assign classroom tasks so that every student has a part in the success of the class?

- How can I help students feel a sense of belonging and maintain an orderly classroom at the same time?

- How can I offer team-building activities that will make it easy for students to cooperate with each other?

- How can I prevent conflicts among my students?

- How can I intervene in a student conflict in such a way that students are in accord with each other afterward?

- How can I be sure that I call on every student during class discussions?

- How can I provide opportunities that showcase students' strengths?

- How can I involve students in service projects that will help others who are less fortunate?

- How can I teach conflict resolution skills?

- Offer the entire class a reward when they meet an agreed-on goal.
- Use tangible rewards such as stickers or new pencils.
- Write positive comments on papers.
- Change an onerous chore into a pleasant one by allowing students to work on it together.
- Hold a weekly contest.
- Provide an authentic audience for your students' work.
- Display students' work.
- Have students work on solving a real-life problem.
- Incorporate students' interests as often as possible.
- Chart small successes so that students can see that small successes create large ones.
- Encourage students to compliment their classmates.
- End class with an intriguing riddle, poem, or question.
- Take photos of your students while they are working.
- Have students teach class material to each other.
- Bring in interesting objects for students to use as part of a lesson.
- Play games.
- Arrange for students to mentor younger students.
- Provide opportunities for peer tutoring.
- Teach a different study skill each day so that students will find it easier to do their work well.
- Use visual demonstrations such as graphic organizers or illustrations to make class work easier to understand.
- Time your students—for example, let them think for thirty seconds before responding to a question.
- Give students puzzles to solve.
- Give clues about the answer to a question slowly, one clue at a time.
- Have students wear fictional name tags related to the lesson.
- Have students sort items into categories.

6-7 Suggestions on Using Rewards and Praise Effectively

Although it is important to create a supportive classroom environment, many teachers mistakenly rely mainly on rewards and praise to do this. While these are useful tools, they are not easy to manage well. If you would like to improve the way that you use rewards and praise in your class, follow these suggestions:

Rewards

- Do not use food as a reward. It is not a sound educational practice, for many reasons, including the current epidemic of childhood obesity and the possibility that some students may have serious illnesses or allergies that are linked to food.
- Consider the message you send when you reward students with a pass that exempts them from homework.
- Using tangible rewards works best when students know about them in advance and can anticipate earning them.
- To be meaningful, rewards should be infrequent enough to be novel; in addition, they should be appropriate to the task.
- Tangible rewards work best when used in combination with intrinsic motivation.

Praise

- Praise evaluates and judges a child, effort, or product. Be aware of the implications of praise, and use it judiciously.
- Don't overdo it when you praise students. If you are too effusive or flattering, students will not take you seriously.
- Be sure that you don't play favorites.
- Praise genuinely difficult accomplishments. If you praise students for routine successes, they might feel insulted at your low expectations.
- Be sensitive about how you praise students. Some prefer private recognition.
- Be specific in your praise so that students have a clear understanding of what they did right.

- Ribbon
- Bookmark
- Extra computer time
- Sticker
- Photograph of the student with his or her work
- Mention on the class Web page
- Mention in the school announcements
- Banner
- Being line leader
- Leaving class first
- Sitting at the teacher's desk
- Decorated desk
- Having work published
- Leading a class game
- Wearing a badge
- Playing trash can basketball
- Praise of student in phone call to student's home
- Sitting with a friend
- Playing a computer game
- Drawing on the chalkboard
- Eating outside
- Listening to music while working
- A personal note from you

- Certificate
- Being first in line at lunch
- Sit in class beanbag chair or other comfortable spot
- Trophy
- Freedom to sharpen pencils anytime
- Fun worksheet
- Being voted Student of the Week
- Name on class wall of fame
- Extra credit points
- Sitting at a special table for lunch
- Token money to spend at class store
- Being selected to run errands
- Opportunity to tutor younger students
- Mention in class newsletter
- Small figurine
- School supplies
- More time for independent reading
- Raffle ticket for later drawing
- Hall pass for water fountain break
- Having work displayed

- Although praise can be a useful way to motivate students to do their best, teachers who use encouragement instead find that it is much more effective.

- At its best, encouragement offers sincere and constructive feedback about the work that a student has accomplished.

- Encouragement differs from praise in that its focus is on students' actions rather than on the students themselves. Compare these examples:

  + Praise: "You did a great job on this!"

  + Encouragement: "Your Venn diagram is balanced and complete!"

- Encouragement targets specific behaviors or work. It does not address general issues; rather, it pinpoints small, specific areas.

- Encouragement is a formative assessment whose purpose is to show students how they are doing at the moment. Effective encouragement deals not just with the outcome but with the actions that students had to take to reach that outcome. In the following example, achievement is linked to the behavior that the student had to accomplish to succeed.

  + Encouragement: "I can tell by these correct answers that your practice has paid off."

- Whereas praise might label a child with terms such as "superstar" or "brilliant," encouragement does not. Instead, the focus remains on the work and not on the personal characteristics of the child.

- Encouragement creates a risk-free environment in which students learn to control their own success and thus become lifelong learners.

6-10 Suggestions for Incorporating Intrinsic Motivation in Instruction

Intrinsic motivation differs from extrinsic motivation in that there are no tangible rewards for effort or achievement; the work itself is so inherently compelling that students are motivated to work.

- Have students take responsibility for part of the instruction. Have them write test questions, offer suggestions for what to include in a review, or even teach part of the lesson.

- Challenge students to beat their personal best on an assignment.

- Create fast-paced assignments so that students will move quickly through their work.

- Provide frequent assessments so that students know exactly what they have to do to succeed. Frequent assessments also hold them accountable for their work.

- Show models of good work from other students so that students will know not only what to do but what that classmate did to succeed.

- Hold periodic conferences with your students in order to discuss problems, progress, and successes.

- Differentiate instruction so that students at different levels will feel comfortable and successful as they work.

- Provide opportunities for students to use their imagination and creativity as often as possible. Design instruction that involves questions such as "And then what?" or "So what?" If students are required to produce a final product as a result of their imaginative work, they will work even harder.

- Pace instruction so that the successful completion of one assignment is dependent on another. This practice will add instant credibility and importance to the first assignment.

CHAPTER 7

Take a Proactive Stance to Prevent Misbehavior

7-1 Be Prepared: Know Why Students Misbehave

You will find it easier to prevent students from misbehaving if you can determine the reasons for the misconduct. Once you know what caused the misbehavior, you can work with students to solve the problem. When your students misbehave, they

* Are testing boundaries
* Don't feel a connection with you
* Want attention from you, classmates, or their families
* Have been upset by an event in another classroom
* Are bored with the assignment
* Don't believe they can do the work and have given up
* Have finished their work early and want to amuse themselves
* Do not place a value on education
* Are upset by something that happened at home
* Perceive the work as too easy or too hard
* Are excited about an upcoming event
* Have assignments that are incompatible with their learning styles
* Need a refresher course in school citizenship
* Are distracted by something or someone near them
* Do not have realistic goals
* Are uncertain about how to do the assignment
* Have no effective positive or negative consequences
* Weren't paying attention when you gave directions
* Couldn't hear you because the class was too noisy
* Don't feel well
* Are having conflicts with peers
* Don't feel a sense of ownership in the class
* Would rather be thought cool than dumb
* Do not think the work is relevant or meaningful

* Greet students at the door, to make sure they know what they must do to accomplish the opening exercise.

* Motivate students to work instead of misbehave by differentiating learning activities to appeal to various learning styles.

* Provide structured exercises at the close of class instead of allowing free time.

* When you introduce a new activity, be sure to thoroughly explain not just the work but also the behavior you expect.

* Create opportunities for success at the start of a unit of study so that students will be motivated to continue.

* Make sure your students know that you like being with them and have confidence in their ability to accomplish what you ask them to do.

* Learn to say no in a calm, pleasant, straightforward way.

* Break up long lessons into small increments of time so that students will be able to remain focused.

* Allow plenty of practice opportunities so that students will gain confidence and stay on task.

* Refer to students' long-term and short-term goals so students have a purpose for working.

* Build reading success strategies into every lesson. When students read well, they begin a cycle of success that engenders good behavior along the way.

* Catch them being good. Praise students when they behave well if you want their good behavior to continue.

* Be strict. There is nothing wrong with being a strict teacher. There is everything wrong with being a mean teacher.

Although it is not always easy to know what to do to prevent discipline problems, some mistakes are clear-cut. Good teachers *don't*

* State the rules of the class in negative instead of positive language
* React to a problem without pausing to consider the cause
* Give up on difficult students
* Begin giving instructions before they have everyone's attention
* Punish a group for the misbehaviors of some
* Allow disagreeable students to sleep because they are not bothering anyone when they are asleep
* Lose their temper
* Allow a student to be rude to them or to classmates
* Assign consequences that are not suitable for the misconduct
* Threaten, nag, cajole, or shout
* Have low expectations for student success
* Arrange classroom furniture and equipment awkwardly, causing traffic flow problems
* Play favorites by allowing some students to be an exception to class rules
* Embarrass a student in front of the class
* Wait until behavior has become serious before calling a student's parents or asking for help from other supportive adults
* Make it difficult for students to be successful by neglecting to use state-mandated guidelines to organize instruction
* Enforce class rules inconsistently
* Allow free time
* Rush to send students to the office too quickly
* Refuse to enforce school rules and policies that they don't care for

7-4 Support Student Self-Management

The ultimate goal for all teachers, regardless of the age of their students, is for their students to learn to successfully regulate their own behavior. When students become self-disciplined, teachers have the opportunity to focus on learning instead of crowd control. Try the following tips to help your students learn to take charge of their own behavior.

* Give explicit directions. In order to remain on task, students need to know exactly what to do.

* Hold class discussions to make sure that you and your students have the same idea of what constitutes acceptable behavior and what does not.

* Make students aware of their own behaviors so that they can monitor themselves. Here's how:

    + Select a few behaviors that you would like to increase.

    + Display a large graph to track the frequency of these positive behaviors.

    + At the end of class each day, spend a few moments evaluating and recording your students' performance.

    + End each session by asking, "What did you do well today, and what can you do better tomorrow?"

* Teach social skills and appropriate ways to deal with peer conflicts when necessary.

* Raise awareness of the importance of self-management through frequent feedback. Praise students who take responsibility for their own actions.

* Make it easy for your students to contact you about concerns and suggestions they may have. Consider using a suggestion box, individual conferences, e-mail, or exit tickets to keep lines of communication open.

7-5 Make Things Run Smoothly with Classroom Procedures

Students who follow classroom procedures are less likely to misbehave than those who don't. Make your classroom a place where things function smoothly by teaching classroom procedures for specific routine tasks or events.

Your students will need to know how to

* Complete start-of-class routines
* Manage book bags and other personal belongings
* Manage cell phones
* Handle tardiness
* Obtain materials and supplies
* Use shared class supplies
* Sharpen pencils
* Signal for the teacher's attention
* Respond when the teacher signals for attention
* Manage acceptable talk during seatwork
* Control noise levels
* Organize their notebooks
* Distribute handouts
* Head papers with the appropriate information
* Turn in papers
* Record homework in an assignment notebook
* Complete homework correctly
* Complete makeup work
* Turn in late work
* Discuss a concern about a grade
* Correct their papers
* Move into groups
* Behave during a small-group discussion

- Behave during a whole-group discussion
- Use computers appropriately
- View videos or television
- Ask classmates for help
- Ask the teacher for help
- Behave when there is a guest
- Behave during a fire or disaster drill
- Ask to leave the room before the end of class
- Complete end-of-class routines

7-6　Enforce Your School's Code of Conduct

Many experienced teachers complain when their colleagues, particularly new teachers, miss opportunities to promote good behavior because they do not consistently enforce the school's code of conduct—the rules, policies, and procedures that apply to every student. If you and all of your fellow teachers united in consistent enforcement for the good of the entire school, there would be many benefits:

- ❋ Your supervisors and colleagues would regard you as someone who takes professional responsibilities seriously.

- ❋ Teachers would not have to repeatedly correct the same mistakes.

- ❋ Students would stop testing the boundaries of acceptable behavior because those boundaries would be clear.

- ❋ You would have more time and energy to enjoy your students.

- ❋ Students and parents would not fault your judgment because you are enforcing an agreed-on schoolwide rule, policy, or procedure.

To become a teacher who unites with colleagues to enforce the code of conduct for the good of everyone, follow these guidelines:

- ❋ Make sure you have a clear understanding of the rules, policies, and procedures that you are supposed to enforce.

- ❋ Follow the code of conduct yourself. If you don't, students will rightly claim that your actions are unfair.

- ❋ Make time to teach the code of conduct to your students so that they know what is expected of them.

- ❋ Take time to connect your school's rules, policies, and procedures to meaningful real-life experiences so that students can see their purpose.

7-7 Create and Teach Classroom Rules

To create classroom rules, consider these tips:

* To be effective, classroom rules must be
  + Broad enough to cover a wide range of misbehaviors.
  + Always stated in positive terms. (Try "Be respectful of others" instead of "No hitting.")
  + Simple enough that all students can understand and recall them.
  + In agreement with school and district policies.
  + Easy to enforce with reasonable, appropriate, and effective consequences.
* Here are some classroom rules that other teachers have found effective and that fit the criteria for effectiveness:
  + Do your work well.
  + Be respectful of others.
  + Use class time wisely.
  + Follow school rules.
  + Be prepared for class every day.

Here are some ideas on how to teach classroom rules:

* Many teachers find that allowing students a strong voice in creating class rules and consequences builds team spirit and student ownership of the classroom.
* Not only should you create a poster-sized version of your class rules, but you should give each student a copy as well as send a copy home.
* Briefly discussing the rules with students daily for the first three weeks of school helps students understand and follow them.
* Ask students to restate the rules in their own words and give examples of situations that fit each one.

7-8 Strategies to Help You Enforce Classroom Rules

* Don't have classroom rules that you are not comfortable enforcing. Each one should help students mature academically and behaviorally.

* Always try to determine the reason that a student breaks a rule before you assign consequences.

* When a student misbehaves, relate the rule to the behavior by asking the misbehaving student to tell you which rule was broken.

* Be consistent. Your students will behave better and perceive you as fair if you are consistent in how you enforce rules.

* Before you enforce rules, plan your response. Forethought will make it easy for you to choose the best course of action.

* The consequences you assign should be proportional to the infraction. For example, whispering requires a warning. Persistent loud talking requires a home contact.

* Involve students in determining the consequences of breaking the rules. At the start of the term, ask them to suggest ways to handle broken rules.

* Keep consequences simple and establish an escalating hierarchy of consequences such as these:

  + First offense: warning

  + Second offense: phone call or note home

  + Third offense: after-school detention

* Don't forget that rewards, encouragement, and praise are consequences too. Use these valuable tools to focus on positive behavior.

* Make it a point to tell your students when they are following the rules just as often as you tell them when they are not.

✳ Be positive as you monitor. Remember that you should help students, not try to catch them misbehaving.

✳ Keep moving. It is almost impossible to monitor all of your students while you are seated. As you circulate, be careful to make contact with every student.

✳ Arrange a system so that students who need help from you can get it. Some teachers have students put their name on the board, take a number, or use a desk sign.

✳ Write a fact on the board, and ask students to add related facts to it as they finish.

✳ Have students who finish their work early put their name on the board as someone who can help classmates.

✳ Ask students to have their work ready to show you as you go by their desk. Put a check mark on it to indicate that you have seen it.

✳ Have students put stickers on their work once they reach a specific point.

✳ Set a timer or put a finish time on the board so that students can self-monitor the way they use class time.

✳ Arrange desk signs with your students so that they can let you know how they are doing. Here are some that other teachers have found effective:

  ✦ Signs with thumbs-up and thumbs-down pictures

  ✦ Green, red, and yellow desk signs

  ✦ Signs with smiley and frowny faces

  ✦ Question mark sign

✳ Teach students to monitor their own behavior while working in groups. They can assess how well they are working together, how noisy they are, or how much progress they are making.

7-10   How to Redirect Students Who Are Off Task

Long gone are the days when teachers shouted across the room to demand that their students get back to work. Today's savvy teachers employ a wide repertoire of techniques to keep their students focused on productive learning. When you notice students who are off task, try these suggestions:

- Write reminders on sticky notes and put them on the desks of students who are off task.
- Set a timer and give everyone a two-minute break. When the timer buzzes, students can go back to work refreshed.
- Change the pace of the assignment.
- Ask students whether they would like help from a classmate.
- Use your "teacher look" to remind students to keep working.
- Call the student's parent if several attempts to redirect are not successful.
- Remind students of their long-term and short-term goals.
- Ask students to restate your directions.
- Ask students to estimate how long it will take to finish the assignment.
- Count "one, two, three," and wait for everyone to pay attention to your directions.
- Ask students who are struggling with an assignment whether they need help.
- Move to stand near the students who are off task.
- Have students stand, stretch, and then return to work.
- Put your hand on the desk of a student whose attention seems to be wandering.
- Discreetly remove distractions.
- Ask children who are off task to sit near you.
- Pleasantly remind students of the behavior you would like to see in the future.

7-11   Strategies to Prevent Cheating

Because reports indicate that cheating is on the rise in all grades, teachers must be proactive in their approach to preventing cheating. Here are some strategies to help you create a classroom culture in which students do not feel the need to cheat:

* Bring cheating out into the open by talking with your students about your expectations. Discuss your school's policy so that students are aware of the repercussions of cheating.

* Establish a class honor code. To build ownership, allow students a strong voice in creating the code.

* Some students cheat because they lack confidence in their academic skills. Work with them to build their self-esteem.

* Make sure that students have enough time to complete assignments. Be as flexible about due dates as you can.

* If students copy others' homework assignments, rethink the assignments. Design assignments that allow students to work together or give quizzes on the material.

* Have sensible testing protocols. For example, students should cover their test paper, put electronic devices away, and not talk. You should make multiple versions of a test and monitor carefully throughout the testing period.

* Teach students about plagiarism so they understand when they are cheating.

* Make sure your students know that you are aware of the various ways they might cheat. If they know that you are alert, they will be less likely to cheat.

* Know your students and their work. You will be able to recognize a copied answer quickly if you are familiar with your students' work.

7-12 Strategies for Creating Successful Seating Charts

❋ To learn your students' names, create an alphabetical seating chart. First, use a sticky note to number each desk. Then, place a number next to each name on your class roster. When students arrive, greet them and direct them to their numbered seats.

❋ One good way to manage a seating chart is to place student names on small sticky notes that fit each square on your seating chart. Slip the entire chart into a plastic page protector to hold the names in place until you want to change them.

❋ After you know your students' names, you should create a seating chart based on their needs.

+ Students with Individualized Education Programs or 504 plans may have plans that require preferential seating for them. For example, students with behavioral problems may need to sit near the teacher.

+ Students who have trouble seeing the board need to sit near the front.

+ Talkative students should either sit together, if they are mature enough to manage their talking, or be separated.

+ Easily distracted students need to sit in an area of the room with few distractions.

+ Students who need extra encouragement need to sit close to you.

❋ Avoid making these mistakes when you create a seating chart:

+ Moving students without considering physical or academic requirements

+ Assigning students to desks that are not the right size for them

+ Seating students based on gender or ethnicity

+ Moving misbehaving students in haste or anger

7-13   Help Students Make Successful Transitions

With a bit of planning, you can reinforce the day's lesson with enjoyable transition activities such as brainteasers, puzzles, or games. Ask students to

* Explain the day's objectives
* Summarize the lesson with a partner
* Fill in the blanks in an outline
* Apply the lesson to real life
* Match words and meanings
* Explain what they learned in the lesson
* Read a brief article and respond to it
* Decide how they will complete their homework
* Brainstorm as many _____s as they can
* Put events in order
* Paraphrase
* Create a cause-and-effect diagram
* Respond to a picture or cartoon
* Predict an outcome
* Scan the text to find . . .
* Locate places on a map
* Use key terms from the lesson in a sentence
* Justify the reasons for . . .
* Quiz themselves on the lesson vocabulary
* Create a graphic organizer
* Highlight key words in their notes
* Draw a concept from the lesson
* Create a true-or-false quiz
* Write a question about the next day's lesson
* List important facts from the lesson
* Explain why the day's lesson is useful
* Explain a study skill related to the lesson

* Write a word such as *SUCCESS* on the board, and set a goal such as 100 percent homework completion. When students achieve their goal for the day, circle one of the letters. When the entire word is circled, celebrate with a small reward.

* Share odd facts, surprising statistics, and other intriguing information about the material in the lesson.

* Keep everyone alert by tossing a soft ball to students as you call on them.

* Wear a silly hat or costume related to the lesson.

* Ask students to create their own board games and then play them.

* Play icebreaker games all year long.

* Randomly place stickers on handouts before you distribute them so that students with the stickers can be surprised with a bonus point.

* Establish celebration routines such as a class finger-snapping pattern or victory dance.

* Play simple games such as Twenty Questions or bingo.

* Hold a brainteaser or riddle contest every week.

* Hold a raffle for school supplies. Students can earn tickets for good behavior.

* Tweak an ordinary lesson to make it more fun. For example, instead of just drawing a picture of a historical figure, have students make the drawing while blindfolded.

* Have students create a question about the lesson that will stump their classmates.

* Allow wiggle breaks every fifteen minutes. Play Simon Says to help everyone stretch.

CHAPTER 8

Minimize Disruptions Caused by Misbehavior

◆ Your first priority is to make sure that all of your students are safe at all times.

◆ Prevent as much misbehavior as you can by cultivating a finely tuned awareness of what is happening in your classroom at any given moment.

◆ You should handle most of the discipline problems in your classroom yourself. Refer students to an administrator for serious issues only.

◆ Students with special needs, young students, and students with behavior problems require more careful supervision than others.

◆ Consistently and fairly enforce school and classroom rules, policies, and procedures.

◆ The consequences for classroom misbehaviors must be appropriate to the offense.

◆ You are expected to keep accurate records of behavior incidents and interventions for all students.

◆ Don't tempt students by leaving personal belongings, money, or test keys where they could be stolen.

◆ All students have the right to due process.

◆ You are expected to cooperate with parents, guardians, administrators, and all other support personnel to help children succeed behaviorally.

◆ Be careful to anticipate safety and behavior issues when you plan instruction. Be especially aware of activities in which students are in competition or engaged in activities that involve a loosely structured environment.

◆ Never leave students unsupervised.

◆ Acquaint yourself with the basics of school law so that you know how to handle misbehavior in the most beneficial way.

Behaviors That You Can Ignore

You can ignore misbehaviors that are brief, self-corrected, or involve only one or two students. Examples include

- Not paying attention
- Talking hushed by other students
- Daydreaming
- Whispering quietly

Behaviors That Require a Mild Warning or Reminder

These behaviors tend to be ones that are the result of impulsivity, high energy, or boundary testing. Examples include

- Talking too loudly
- Off-task conversation
- Failure to finish work
- Lack of materials
- Passing notes
- Minor procedure violations
- Extended daydreaming
- Brief, friendly horseplay
- Occasional tardiness

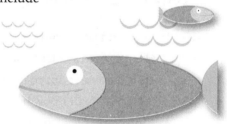

Behaviors That Require Negative Consequences

These behaviors generally interfere with learning and require negative consequences or help from a parent or guardian. Examples include

- Serious horseplay
- Rudeness
- Refusal to work
- Repeated procedure violations
- Defiance
- Talking back
- Minor vandalism
- Eating or drinking in class

Sometimes consistent enforcement is not enough to create a lasting change in student behavior. Before you react in anger and punish students, consider a problem-solving approach.

Why Punishment Does Not Succeed

- It focuses on the past.
- It does not further your relationship with your students.
- It doesn't build self-discipline or enhance skills in conflict resolution.
- It sets a negative tone for your interactions.
- Your reaction could create a ripple of unpleasant emotions in the classroom.

Why Problem Solving Does Succeed

- You and your students work cooperatively to improve a situation.
- It improves student competence and conflict resolution skills.
- It is a positive approach that can be applied to other areas of life.
- Students will know how they are supposed to act in the future.
- Your positive response will earn your students' respect and trust.

How to Work with Students to Solve Problems

- *Step One:* Talk with the student to agree on exactly what happened and the reasons for the misbehavior. Be open and straightforward, and don't accept excuses.
- *Step Two:* Work with the student to generate several possible solutions that will keep the problem from reoccurring. Write each one down.
- *Step Three:* Talk the possible solutions over in order to select one or two that could prevent future misbehavior.
- *Step Four:* Discuss what you both should do if the misbehavior occurs again.
- *Step Five:* Agree to work together to implement your plan.

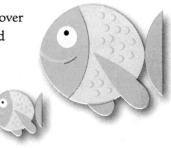

8-4 General Strategies to Minimize Disruptions

Sometimes students misbehave despite our careful plans and efforts to prevent misbehavior from starting. When this happens, it is your responsibility to minimize the disruption so that its negative impact on the learning environment is negligible. Try these suggestions to keep misbehaviors small and manageable:

- Be alert to the early signs of misbehavior. Ignore as much as you can.

- Intervene quickly once you see a need.

- Be decisive. Plan how you are going to handle misbehavior, and act on your plans.

- Remain calm. If you overreact, you will only make things worse.

- Quietly ask wrongdoers whether they need help.

- Move students away from the cause of their misbehavior and their audience.

- Do your best to keep teaching or to make sure that other students keep working on their assignment.

- If the misbehavior is minor, praise nearby students who are behaving well.

- Move closer to the student. Give a warning in a quiet voice.

- Arrange a plan for timeouts with another teacher so that students can have a chance to cool off and control themselves.

- Enforce your rules, using the tiers of consequences you have established.

- Choose to delay acting on the bad behavior until other students have settled down to work.

- Call a parent or guardian so that you can work together on solving a behavior problem.

- Don't forget that you are the responsible adult in the room and that it is your responsibility to determine the disposition of a problem.

8-5 Be Alert to the Potential for Violence

Violent behavior at school can take many forms. Because it is your responsibility to keep students safe and to lessen the disruption when an incident occurs, you must be alert to the potential for all types of violence at school. When you notice any of the following signs, be aware that they often precede more serious problems.

- Students who bully a classmate
- Frequent absences
- Students who appear depressed
- Students who are experiencing relationship issues with a boyfriend or girlfriend
- Substance abuse by a student
- Substance abuse in a student's home
- A student being bullied or picked on
- Teasing, name calling, or verbal taunts
- An argument in the community or in another class
- Students who cut class
- Reports of cyber-bullying
- Students who are isolated from classmates
- Horseplay
- Frequent lies or excuses
- Excessive interest in weapons
- Frequent references to violent video games or other violent media
- Student reports of threats
- Notes with threats or references to violence
- Students with a past history of violence
- Defiance of authority
- Student reports of a weapon
- Graffiti
- Students who are gang members
- Obscene gestures
- A higher overall energy level in your class
- Overly intense reactions to minor conflicts

8-6　How to Respond When Students Fight

Conflicts that escalate into a fight can happen at any school. You need to be aware of what you should do when a fight breaks out so that you are prepared to respond.

- Thoroughly familiarize yourself with your school district's procedures for handling student fights. When a fight breaks out, you will need to think quickly.

- You must intervene, but when you do, be extremely careful. Fights are dangerous for bystanders as well as for combatants.

  - Do your best to stop the fighting and disperse the crowd, so that no one is injured.

  - Do not try to step between the students in a fight without another adult present. If you touch a student in the midst of a fight, you risk being injured yourself or causing that student to be hurt.

- Send students for help. Do not leave the area yourself.

- If students are injured, get medical attention for them at once. If you are hurt, report your injuries.

- Monitor your own adrenaline level. You should appear calm in front of students.

- Confiscate any weapons; your school's security officer will need them.

- Jot down accurate notes about the incident. You may need to refer to them later, if charges are filed.

- After a fight is over, calm the crowd and get them back to work or play. Be matter-of-fact in order to settle the crowd quickly.

8-7 How to Refer Students to an Administrator

One of the toughest decisions you will have to make when students misbehave is whether to refer them to an administrator for further disciplinary action. Use the following suggestions to ensure that the referrals you make are productive ones that can successfully resolve the problem.

- Make sure that you have copies of the referral form handy so that you can act promptly.

- Remain calm. Your goal is to minimize disruption. If you can delay making the referral until the end of class, try to do so.

- Because many different people will see the referral form, you must fill it out carefully. Be objective and succinct. Do not refer to other students by name.

- If the problem is one that has been persistent, talk it over with an administrator before you make the referral. Provide documentation of the interventions you have attempted.

- After you make a referral, follow up with the administrator to clarify any possible confusion.

- Once you have referred a student, accept the decisions of the administrator, even if you do not fully agree with them.

- The following behaviors are severe enough to require that you involve an administrator:

  - Persistent disruptions
  - Violent behavior
  - Threats
  - Using weapons
  - Cheating
  - Gang activity
  - Bullying
  - Destruction of property
  - Deliberate profanity
  - Substance abuse

Why It's Important to Maintain Your Self-Control

◆ You'll keep misbehaviors small and in perspective.

◆ It will protect the dignity of the misbehaving student.

◆ It will be easier to resolve the problem if you are composed.

◆ Attention will be on the problem and not on your reaction to it.

◆ Overreacting might damage your relationship with the misbehaving student.

◆ Losing control will hurt your credibility with students, your supervisors, and parents or guardians.

◆ Losing your temper will not add to the positive class atmosphere you want for your students.

◆ Even students who are not involved in the incident could be unfairly intimidated by your lack of self-control.

◆ As an adult role model, you will feel foolish and remorseful later if you lose control.

How to Control Your Reactions When Students Misbehave

◆ Lower your voice. You will appear calm even if you are not, and everyone will have to quiet down to listen to you.

◆ Mentally count to ten. Count some more if you are still not in control of yourself. Take several deep breaths, and exhale slowly.

◆ Remind yourself of the reasons that it is important to stay calm.

◆ Be prepared. Have a plan already in place for dealing with misbehavior.

◆ Delay acting for even a few moments, if possible. This delay will give you time to collect your thoughts.

◆ Remind yourself that the students who did not misbehave deserve your best.

- What caused the student to misbehave?
- More than one student was involved; how can I be sure that I have a clear understanding of each child's actions and motives?
- What rules should apply?
- Did I refer to or explain the rule that was broken?
- What consequences should apply?
- How can I be sure that the consequences fit the misbehavior and will be effective in preventing a reoccurrence?
- Was the disciplinary action consistent with school and classroom policies?
- Was my personal reaction appropriate?
- Did I minimize the disturbance the incident caused?
- Did I act quickly enough?
- Was any student in danger? If so, what can I do to ensure that student's safety in the future?
- Did I handle it fairly? Do my students think that I was fair?
- Did I take a problem-solving approach?
- Did I involve school personnel and parents or guardians quickly enough? Why or why not?
- How can I help my student move toward self-disciplined behavior?
- Could I have predicted this misbehavior?
- What will I do if it happens again?
- How can I have a positive relationship with this student?
- Did I address the underlying reasons for the behavior?
- Did I treat the misbehaving student with compassion, dignity, and respect?
- How can I focus on and develop the positive attributes of this student?
- How could I have handled it better?
- What lessons did I learn that I can use in the future?

Section Three

Be a Dynamic Teacher

Becoming a dynamic teacher is one of the most worthwhile goals that any educator can have, and it does not happen by accident. To create an active classroom in which students self-manage their progress as they work with purpose, you will need to master three key components of instruction. In this section, you will learn how to design, deliver, and assess effective and appropriate instruction that will help you and your students reach your goals.

IN CHAPTER NINE, you will find the up-to-date techniques, activities, and strategies you need to design instruction that invites and empowers your students to become active partners in their learning.

IN CHAPTER TEN, the focus is on classroom-proven strategies to help you present lessons that are so appealing, relevant, and effective that your students will be motivated toward success. From harnessing the power of your enthusiasm to gearing instruction toward your students' preferred learning styles, using the beginning and ending of class for instruction, and increasing retention through review, you will learn how to make each lesson meaningful and productive.

IN CHAPTER ELEVEN, you will learn about types of assessments and the advantages of each. You will also learn techniques for giving constructive feedback, keeping up with grading paperwork, and helping your students succeed on standardized tests.

CHAPTER 9

Plan Effective Instruction

9-1 Your Goal: An Active Learning Community

You will know that your strategies for planning effective instruction have been effective when you notice these results in your classroom:

- Students working to achieve state and district objectives

- Differentiated activities that appeal to every student's ability level and preferred learning style

- Students engaged in decision making, inquiry, problem solving, and open-ended activities

- Appropriate support for all students, including those with special needs

- A teacher using monitoring, coaching, and collaboration to facilitate instruction and assist students

- Students working with their teacher to assess and track their own progress

- High expectations that apply to every student

- Students using classroom rules, procedures, and schedules to govern themselves

- Students working cooperatively with their teacher and their classmates to plan and direct their own work

- Students who are motivated to work by means of individual and group incentives in addition to grades

- Groups of students of mixed ability levels working together on real-world, meaningful assignments

- Students who are not afraid to take risks because the atmosphere is inclusive and encouraging

- Students engaging in enthusiastic discussions in which the noise level may be high but is the result of productivity and engagement

- Evidence that the instructor has completed careful planning and preparation

9-2 Steps in Planning Instruction

STEP ONE: Begin by downloading objectives, ancillary materials, and other resources from your state's department of education Web site and your school district's Web site.

STEP TWO: Examine textbooks and other materials that your school offers, in order to find resources and support as you plan instruction that will meet state and district standards.

STEP THREE: Carefully review both the material you have downloaded and the information in your school's resources in order to create a course overview. Begin by determining the required knowledge and essential skills that are most important for your students to master.

STEP FOUR: Decide how to group both knowledge and skills into units of study. Then, create a course timeline in order to schedule these essential elements.

STEP FIVE: Determine the materials, activities, and strategies you will use to teach each unit. At this point, you should also plan the assessments that you will use to evaluate your students' progress. Many teachers find it helpful to write a brief outline of each unit at the start of the year and add the details later.

STEP SIX: Write your daily plans. Begin by asking yourself these questions:

+ How will today's lesson help students reach the course goals?
+ What is the most effective way to teach the content in this lesson?

STEP SEVEN: After each lesson, make notes about what went well and how you can improve the next time you teach it. Add these notes to your plans.

STEP ONE: Select the topic that you want to teach as a unit of study. Divide it into smaller concepts and skill sets that you expect students to master. Even though your instructional methods may vary according to students' abilities and learning preferences, have the same high expectations for content mastery for all students.

STEP TWO: Research the topic to determine the indispensable content as well as the content you would like to treat as remedial or enrichment material.

STEP THREE: Write down the essential questions that students will strive to answer as they study the material.

STEP FOUR: Assess your students' prior knowledge to determine the most appropriate activities to help them reach content mastery.

STEP FIVE: Determine the length of time that you intend to allot to this unit of study, being careful to allow for unforeseen circumstances such as an inclement weather day.

STEP SIX: Plan a variety of activities that will appeal to as many students' ability levels, learning styles, and interests as possible. Be sure to include

+ Motivational activities to pique student interest
+ Alternative activities that will appeal to students who need remediation or enrichment
+ Activities that will appeal to students with various learning styles
+ Anchoring activities that students can work on independently as the unit progresses

STEP SEVEN: Write tests, quizzes, and other assessments that you will use to evaluate your students' progress. Writing assessments before you teach the material will clarify and focus your instructional goals.

Instead of using a traditional plan book, many teachers have found it efficient to create an electronic template for writing daily plans. Not only does that make it easy to adjust plans, but they can also be printed and stored in a binder for quick reference. Whatever method you use to write your plans, effective daily lesson plans should contain the following basic components:

- ❑ *Objectives:* The goals that all instructional activities are designed to achieve
- ❑ *Materials:* The resources and equipment necessary for the lesson
- ❑ *Prior knowledge assessments:* Methods that will be used to determine student readiness for the material in the lesson
- ❑ *Essential questions:* Far-reaching questions that promote enduring knowledge
- ❑ *Anticipatory sets:* Opening exercises designed to arouse interest and activate background knowledge
- ❑ *Teacher input:* The instruction that you provide directly to students
- ❑ *Guided practice:* Activities that students will perform with your assistance
- ❑ *Independent practice:* Activities that students will perform without your assistance
- ❑ *Alternative assignments:* Activities that are needed to differentiate instruction
- ❑ *Closure:* Activities designed to reinforce the day's learning
- ❑ *Assessments:* Evaluation procedures used to determine student progress
- ❑ *Homework:* Additional assignments that arise naturally from the lesson
- ❑ *Reflection:* The thinking that you do about the lesson and the notes that you make about it after the lesson is finished

Students learn more efficiently when they can connect new learning with previous knowledge. Use the suggestions in the following list to give students confidence and arouse their interest as they approach new material.

- Ask students to write for two minutes in response to an open-ended question about the material.

- Have students survey their classmates about key issues in the content.

- Show a video clip or ask students to listen to an audio clip, and then ask for a response.

- Ask students to write a one-sentence summary of what they already know about the topic.

- Give a brief pretest in which students can respond with fill-in-the-blank or matching answers.

- Have students respond to a question about the topic with a quick sketch.

- Ask students to brainstorm words related to the topic and share their lists, first with a partner and then with the entire class.

- Give students a series of statements about the material and ask them to indicate whether they agree or disagree with the statements, find them to be true or false, or believe them to be facts or opinions.

- Have students complete a graphic organizer such as a cluster map, Venn diagram, or KLW (Know-Learned-Want to Know) chart.

- Display items such as maps, books, tools, documents, or other objects related to the topic, and ask for a response.

- Ask students to discuss the topic for one minute with a partner and then share what they know with the rest of the class.

9-6 Adapt Instruction to Meet the Needs of All Learners

- Each learner is different. Teachers need to respond by offering a range of activities that will allow students with different learning preferences to process and acquire information successfully

- There are two areas of curriculum to differentiate:

  - *Process:* Although all students should be held to the same high expectations for mastery, content acquisition should be the result of multiple and varied approaches. Students should be able to choose from a range of activities that appeal to their different readiness levels, interests, and learning styles as they study new information.

  - *Products:* All students should have a variety of ways to apply and demonstrate their learning through assessments and products.

- Teachers must be willing to modify instruction instead of expecting all students to conform to one learning style. This approach requires open-minded, flexible teachers.

- Teachers use a variety of assessments on an ongoing basis to identify students' learning styles and learning preferences and to optimize their teaching to take advantage of students' preferences.

- Instruction should focus on understanding broad concepts instead of memorizing small collections of facts. Acquisition of enduring knowledge should be the result.

- Activities should include a mixture of group and individual activities that concentrate on higher-order thinking skills.

- Activities should be balanced between teacher-assigned and student-generated assignments.

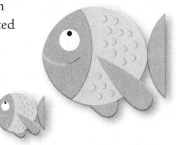

- Covering material is not as important as making it possible for students to understand general concepts.

9-7 Create Enduring Understanding with Essential Questions

Essential questions are thoughtful, open-ended questions that ask students to solve problems or make decisions as they investigate topics involving the human condition. Because of the complex, high-level thinking skills required to answer them, essential questions help students to achieve state standards.

- Although essential questions vary according to students' grade level and the content under study, they share some important traits:

  + Essential questions ask students to consider issues that are large in scope.

  + Essential questions are designed to stimulate thinking, collaboration, research, and discussion.

  + Students must evaluate information and data as they investigate, gather information, and make thoughtful decisions in order to formulate their responses to essential questions.

  + Often one essential question will generate others.

  + Essential questions often deal with controversial topics.

  + Because they are open-ended, essential questions require complex answers that are unique to the students who are working with them.

  + In order to answer essential questions, students must rely not only on content knowledge and research but also on personal experience.

- In many cases, an essential question is posed as a scenario that students are asked to investigate through thoughtful research. For example:

  If you were to design a new public library for our community, what types of services would the library offer? How would you integrate technology? Who would benefit most from your design?

9-8 Include Activities That Will Appeal to Your Students

No matter their age or ability level, your students will find it easy to be engaged in productive learning if you offer them activities that

- Appeal to their interests
- Allow limited choices
- Include frequent checkpoints so that they can monitor their own progress
- Are relevant to students' lives and interests, meaningful, and related to their immediate needs
- Use media and technology
- Allow them to confer with each other
- Are paced appropriately for their readiness to learn
- Include multiple learning modalities
- Involve real-life problems
- Appeal to their sense of fun
- Allow them to help others

Some activities that students enjoy include

- Solving puzzles
- Viewing and making movies
- Role-playing
- Discussions
- Debates
- Brainstorming with partners
- Demonstrations
- Creating mnemonics
- Studying together
- Playing games
- Dramatizations
- Creating graphic organizers
- Interviews

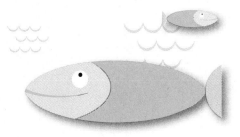

- WebQuests
- Virtual tours
- Deciphering clues
- Practicing with flash cards
- Taking photographs
- Predicting outcomes
- Rapid-fire drills
- Sorting items into categories
- Group activities
- Sketching

9-9 Use Resources That Take Students Beyond the Text

Although the material in the textbook is important, good teachers know that it is only a beginning. Many resources offer information, links to other resources, teaching strategies, and other useful ideas about the content your students are studying. Consider investigating some of these resources to enrich your curriculum:

- Primary source documents
- Various types of maps
- Brochures
- Pamphlets
- Blogs
- Local or regional newspapers
- Foreign newspapers
- Historical newspapers
- Oral histories
- Public service organizations
- Special interest organizations
- News organizations
- Television stations
- Radio stations
- Advertisements
- Pen pals
- Interviews with community members
- Interviews with students
- Surveys
- Video clips
- Audio clips
- Music
- Magazines
- Artifacts
- Autobiographies
- Biographies
- Fictional accounts
- Encyclopedias
- Databases
- Web sites
- Guest speakers
- Field trips
- Virtual field trips
- WebQuests
- Local libraries
- Sports teams
- Celebrities
- Letters to experts
- E-mails to experts
- Local businesses
- Retirement communities
- Government officials
- Government information bulletins
- Museums
- Performances

Although nontraditional schedules have many permutations, the planning process for all of them contains similar requirements. Use these suggestions to make planning more manageable.

- Be sensitive to the optimum attention span of your students. Many learners have difficulty sustaining focused attention for longer than fifteen minutes. Break up long instructional periods into small blocks of time.

- With nontraditional schedules, often students may study a subject in one semester and then not again for months. It is important to help students retain information by improving the connections they make to the material they are studying. With stronger connections, students will find it easier to process and retain new content.

- Beginning class with a review of the previous day's lesson is an excellent way to help students succeed. If students are not in school for several days or even weeks because of a nontraditional schedule, more time must be devoted to review of earlier material.

- It is tempting to plan too many activities when you have longer class periods. Don't overestimate how much time you have. Set a schedule, and stick to it.

- Use a syllabus with older students or a posted schedule with younger ones so that students know what they are expected to achieve and how long they have to work. When students cooperate with their teachers to manage class time efficiently, they can minimize the disadvantages of nontraditional schedules.

9-11   How to Create Backup Plans

One bit of excellent advice that new teachers often hear is that they should have backup plans to use when a lesson isn't working or an unforeseen event interrupts the day's schedule. There are several ways that you can make sure you always have a backup plan:

- Ask other teachers to share their suggestions for backup plans with you.
- When you create alternative plans for enrichment or remediation, consider using some of them as backup plans.
- Take another approach to a lesson. For example, if you have asked students to work independently, allow them to work with a partner.
- Keep a collection of board games on hand.
- Keep a collection of text materials related to your subject or grade level on hand.
- Have students play a review game that uses key terms from the material under study.
- Ask students to illustrate facts on the board, on an overhead transparency, or on paper.
- Read an inspiring article aloud to your students, and ask for their opinions about it.
- Allow students to study together with flash cards, a study guide, or a pretest.
- Have students play educational computer games.
- Have students complete a group activity.
- Post a collection of brief activities that students can choose from when their work is complete or when you need to introduce a change in the day's lesson.
- Have students complete practice items for standardized tests.

Although the best way to adapt a lesson for your students who are less proficient at mastering material quickly is to respond to them as individuals, sometimes you may find that several students are experiencing difficulties. In the following list, you will find some ways to adapt lessons so that all of your students can be successful.

- Be sure to engage every learner in your class by offering activities that allow them to use their preferred learning styles. Varying the learning modalities in a lesson will make it easier for all students to learn.

- Provide more examples, models, and demonstrations so that students know exactly what they are to do and learn.

- Build on what your students already know by showing them how new material relates to what they have already learned.

- Ask students to diagnose what they find difficult about the lesson, and then use this information to adjust the lesson accordingly.

- Build students' self-confidence by encouraging their efforts as well as their achievements.

- Allow students to work with peers in mixed-ability groups.

- Consider shortening the assignment so that the basics are covered but frustrating extra work is not required.

- Supply students with support materials such as word banks and outlines, to make the content more accessible.

- Have students complete graphic organizers, making a visual representation of what they are learning.

- Encourage less-proficient students to use technology for review and practice.

- Sometimes all that is necessary is more time to complete an assignment.

CHAPTER 10

Deliver Effective Instruction

Teachers who enjoy their subjects and their students infuse their teaching with passion, which, in turn, creates interested and enthusiastic learners. Here are several ways that you can use your enthusiasm to create student success:

- Be sure you have a thorough knowledge of the topic so that you can be completely comfortable in teaching it.

- Let your body language project your positive feelings. Eye contact, pleasant facial expressions, a high energy level, and lively speech all convey your zeal.

- Drop hints! Mention that students will enjoy an upcoming topic and that you are looking forward to teaching it.

- If your students use a syllabus or course schedule, you can awaken their interest with a countdown to the topic or thrilling allusions to impending activities.

- Make sure that you have a positive answer ready when a student asks, "Why do we have to know this?"

- Teach intriguing sidelights and fascinating facts related to the day's topic.

- Display posters, quotations, photographs, and other visual materials to reveal your enthusiasm to your students.

- Begin each lesson with an attention grabber. Wear a costume, bring in objects, or sing silly songs—whatever it takes to show that you are eager to teach.

- Relate the content of your lesson to real-life situations so that students will understand the purpose of their learning.

- Make sure that your students know how much you enjoy being with *them*.

- Spend time getting to know your students' culture, experiences, and future plans. By listening carefully, you will be able to present material that is pertinent to their lives, needs, and dreams.

- Some students are not motivated by grades. Find other rewards and recognitions to lend significance to their efforts and achievements.

- Have students set both long-term and short-term goals. Having goals to work toward will help students learn to look for meaning in their assignments.

- Show students how the material is immediately useful to them.

- Show students how the material will be useful to them in the future.

- Make students aware of how mastering one topic will often unlock other topics.

- Teach your students how the information you are teaching has benefited others. Ask them to tell you how it can benefit them.

- Enlarge your classroom. Bring in guest speakers and take students on field trips to learn firsthand how instruction can be applied to their life.

- Ask students to brainstorm ways that the material in the lesson is important or useful.

- Use the material in the lesson to help students make connections to other texts, to past experiences, to their community, and to the world.

- Expose even young students to different types of career-related information so they can learn the importance of their learning in finding a useful occupation.

- Ask students to suggest topics that they would like to learn about. Adopt their suggestions whenever you can.

10-3　How to Build Background Knowledge

Building background knowledge is a crucial element in instruction because it allows students to make sense of new material. Developing background knowledge can be an effective instructional tool if you implement some of these pointers:

- Help students recall past events such as family trips or news events so that they can connect familiar experiences to new learning.

- Ask students about books, magazines, or other material they may have already read about the topic under study.

- Give students a list of words. As you discuss the words, show them how they can apply these words to the new material.

- Provide students with different types of enrichment experiences such as trips to concerts, museums, parks, and libraries.

- Help students understand new content by providing an outline or summary of it before they begin working.

- Preview reading passages or chapters with students to help them comprehend the material when they read it.

- Allow students frequent opportunities to independently read books of their own choosing. Independent reading is an important way for students to broaden their background knowledge.

- Ask students to explain what skills or knowledge they already have that might help them understand the new information. Show them how the new knowledge or skills can add to what they already know.

- Provide a bank of key terms and facts before students begin working with new material so that some of it will be familiar to them.

10-4 Incorporate High-Level Thinking Skills

Since 1956, when Benjamin Bloom first created his famous taxonomy, teachers have used it to involve students in meaningful activities. Most of your instruction should focus on the three highest levels of his cognitive domain analysis: evaluation, synthesis, and analysis.

⚙ **EVALUATION:** Students will use standards to formulate judgments about the quality of information.

Student Actions	Student Products
✦ Prioritize	✦ Investigation
✦ Evaluate	✦ Conclusion
✦ Conclude	✦ Verdict
✦ Justify	✦ Self-evaluation
✦ Criticize	✦ Recommendation

⚙ **SYNTHESIS:** Students will combine ideas and information in a new way.

Student Actions	Student Products
✦ Compose	✦ Solution
✦ Assemble	✦ Prediction
✦ Compile	✦ Newsletter
✦ Construct	✦ Collage
✦ Combine	✦ Invention

⚙ **ANALYSIS:** Students will separate a whole into component elements.

Student Actions	Student Products
✦ Experiment	✦ Chart
✦ Sequence	✦ Graph
✦ Dissect	✦ Spreadsheet
✦ Categorize	✦ Outline
✦ Classify	✦ Diagram

10-5 Gear Your Instruction to Students' Preferred Learning Styles

When you assess your students' preferred learning styles and then use that information to adjust instruction to fit your students' needs, the likelihood of successful learning increases. The information here can help you with this important task.

- Although not all researchers categorize learning styles in the same way, most agree that there are at least three different types of learners:
  - *Visual learners,* who learn best by observing and seeing
  - *Auditory learners,* who learn best by listening and speaking
  - *Tactile or kinesthetic learners,* who learn best by touching and manipulating objects

- A sensible classroom approach to the issue of learning styles would be to inventory students in order to make them aware of their preferred learning styles. Students who know that they are auditory learners, for example, could focus independent activities on listening and speaking.

- Because classes are composed of students with diverse learning styles, you should design activities that combine learning styles as often as possible. Use the following activities as examples in planning activities that will appeal to all of your students. Ask students to
  - Read an intriguing passage, watch a video clip, and participate in a follow-up discussion
  - Hold debates that also involve visual representations and student movement
  - Work with a group to demonstrate a process
  - Brainstorm ideas with a partner and then display their work on a poster
  - Participate in a spelling bee or other active learning game

10-6　Suggestions on How to Use Technology for Instruction

Here are just a few of the ways that *teachers* can use technology:

- E-mail students about assignments and class events
- Present information in an electronic slide show
- Post handouts online for students to complete electronically instead of on paper
- Research and create lesson plans
- Set up a class wiki in which students share information about assignments
- Create a class Web page
- Maintain a reflection log about various lessons that can be electronically shared with colleagues
- Make different versions of tests, quizzes, and other assignments

Here are just a few of the ways that *students* can use technology:

- Listen to or create podcasts
- Go on virtual field trips or visit virtual museums
- Play educational games
- Complete electronic puzzles at game sites
- Learn a word of the day or a fact of the day by searching one of the many databases that offer daily words or facts
- Take digital photos
- Present and publish assignments electronically
- Use spreadsheets to track data
- Create graphs
- Store documents in electronic portfolios
- Study facts, using electronic flash cards
- Complete WebQuests
- Research specific topics on the Internet
- E-mail their teacher to keep up with assignments when absent
- E-mail other students about assignments
- Connect with students in other schools, states, or countries
- Read news articles from foreign newspapers on the Internet

10-7 Tips on Making Effective Electronic Presentations

❑ Keep your purpose in mind. An electronic presentation should be informative and aligned with state standards as well as interesting.

❑ Aim for a presentation that is no longer than fifteen minutes. After that, switch to another activity.

❑ Your slides should only have key points. Avoid excessive verbiage.

❑ Create a catchy opening and a powerful closing to reinforce what your audience has learned.

❑ Practice your presentation just as you would any other speech. Be careful to use it to enhance your topic instead of just reading from slides.

❑ Allow extra time to set up and check equipment.

❑ Have a backup plan ready in case of technical difficulties.

❑ Be careful about the type and amount of clip art and sound effects that you use. Too much of either can be distracting.

❑ Do not violate copyright laws. Make sure you have permission when it is required, and always credit your sources.

❑ Keep fonts simple and readable. Keep the number of fonts to a minimum.

❑ Check your presentation from the back of the room to make sure everyone will be able to read it with ease.

❑ A plain background will make your presentation easy for students to read. Keep colors, backgrounds, and fonts uniform.

❑ Three to five bullet points on a slide is optimum. More than that will overwhelm your audience.

❑ Back up your presentation so that a glitch can't erase hours of your hard work.

- Know your material.

- Begin by focusing your students' attention on you by moving to a specific spot in the room and calling for attention. Wait until you have their attention before speaking.

- Keep presentations brief and purposeful. Begin with a provocative statement, catchy question, or anecdote to capture attention. End with a recap of the most important points.

- Make eye contact, smile, and speak loudly enough to command attention.

- Vary your tone of voice to help your students be good listeners.

- If you give oral instructions, limit them to no more than three or four steps. After you tell students what to do, ask someone to restate the instructions. Students will find it easier to follow oral directions if you refer to a written version you have on display.

- When you use props, do so with pizzazz!

- Make your gestures memorable. Plan them as you would any other part of a presentation.

- Students will focus on what you say if you give them an outline to complete as you speak or offer other ways to help them keep up with your presentation.

- To keep students focused on you, move around the classroom as you speak. Your body language should show that you are confident and enthusiastic about the topic.

- Pay attention to your audience, and adjust your manner of delivery if necessary.

- ❑ Thoroughly proofread every handout for grammatical, factual, and typographical errors.

- ❑ Keep the appearance of your handouts uncluttered and readable. Keep the number of fonts to a minimum.

- ❑ Pay attention to format and spacing. If students are expected to write on the handout, allow plenty of room and provide lines for them.

- ❑ Number each page so that students will be able to stay on track as they work through the handout.

- ❑ Provide space for students to head their papers with their name, the date, and the class or subject.

- ❑ Use text features such as clip art, text boxes, or underlining to emphasize important information.

- ❑ Label each handout with a distinctive title so that students can find it quickly.

- ❑ Make directions easy to find. Use a bold font and place them right before the assignments they refer to.

- ❑ If you are going to grade an assignment, help students focus by including point values.

- ❑ Build students' confidence by adding encouraging notes, hints, reminders, and bits of advice.

- ❑ To capture students' attention, refer to their interests and past or upcoming class events, and use their names in positive ways in examples or questions.

- ❑ If you require students to maintain a notebook, make this task easier by punching holes in handouts before you pass them out.

Although the hands-on experiences of field trips can provide stimulating learning opportunities, they are not to be undertaken without meticulous planning.

- ❑ Every field trip should have a sound educational purpose that is aligned with course objectives.

- ❑ Discuss the trip with supervisors and colleagues to ensure that you have completed the required permission forms. Complete all paperwork related to the trip, and keep it on file.

- ❑ Make sure you have enough chaperones. You will need at least one adult for every ten students.

- ❑ Visit the site beforehand, and work with staff members there to guarantee an authentic, safe, and productive learning experience for your students.

- ❑ Prepare students by exploring the destination's Web site, discussing behavior expectations, and assigning learning activities. Plan post-trip activities and discussions as well.

- ❑ Student safety is a crucial concern. Take a first aid kit, cell phone, contact numbers, and emergency medical forms with you. Teach safety procedures to your students, and institute a buddy system for times when students will be out of your sight.

- ❑ Communicate openly with parents and guardians about the trip. Make sure they are aware of the cost (including any additional expenses), when and where to pick up students after the trip, and the activities that students will be engaged in. Create a phone tree so that parents can contact each other and you, if needed.

One of the most inventive ways that technology is transforming instruction saves time and money, allows students access to up-to-date information, and opens classroom doors to the universe. Students on a virtual field trip can talk with experts and visit thousands of faraway places, including such sites as the inside of a cell or a remote galaxy.

When students take a virtual field trip, they begin by accessing an Internet site devoted to the topic under study. Although many virtual field trips are mainly computer tours, others may offer interactive features such as e-mail access to docents or experts. As students explore the sites on the tour through various links, they can also complete various activities related to the lesson.

○ Even though students don't leave the classroom, successful virtual field trips require extensive planning, preparation, supervision, and structure.

○ When choosing from the vast array of field trip sites, consider these factors:

+ Alignment with course goals

+ Appropriateness for the age and ability levels of your students

+ How you will assess learning

+ How you will monitor student computer use

+ Site content

○ Research the sites that your students will visit. Check all links to make certain that they are suitable for school-related activities. Preview any interactive activities that a site may offer.

○ Some of the activities to consider asking your students to complete include

+ Scavenger or treasure hunts

+ E-mail interviews with scientists and other experts at the site

+ Slide shows

+ Posters

- Observation logs, journals, and firsthand reports
- Maps and time lines
- Graphs, charts, and diagrams
- Group or individual reports
- Scrapbooks or portfolios

- Never assign homework as punishment. In most cases, homework assignments should be a continuation of the day's lesson or a preview of the next one.

- Communicate openly with parents. If you work together to solve homework issues, everyone benefits.

- Make sure to establish a homework routine and stick to it. Students and parents both will appreciate this courtesy.

- Try not to assign homework every day. When you do assign it, however, be sensitive to student workload. Older students should have no more than two hours a night from all classes combined; middle school students should have no more than one hour a night; and younger students should have less than an hour of work.

- Create a routine for announcing homework assignments. Many teachers post it in the same place every day for students to copy, explain it at the beginning of class, ask students to explain it at the end of class, have it on a syllabus, and post it on a class Web page.

- Make homework assignments compelling. Students will complete homework if they see a purpose for the work, if it is interesting, and if it is of a reasonable length.

- Hold students accountable. While you do not have to grade all homework assignments, you should check for completeness or select sample questions or problems to grade.

- Inform your students of the types of homework help that are and are not appropriate when you make assignments. Try to design assignments on which students will find it difficult to cheat.

10-13 Tips on Using Collaborative Activities in Class

○ Begin collaboration by having students work first in partners, then in triads, and then in larger groups as they learn the procedures of group work.

○ You and not your students should determine the composition of groups. Aim for groups of students with mixed ability levels.

○ Teach the procedures for working together. Establish signals to let students know when they are successful, too loud, or off task.

○ Be sure to make the assignment and review rules before students move to their groups so that they can focus on you and not each other.

○ Make the task assignment specific and detailed so that students know what to do to be successful. Give students a checklist of the work they need to accomplish, to keep them on task.

○ Circulate and monitor in order to coach, assist, and encourage.

○ Here are some easy collaborative activities that students can complete with success:

+ Review flash cards
+ Discuss reading passages
+ Read aloud to each other
+ Answer questions as they read a passage
+ Solve a problem
+ Complete a quick computer search
+ Edit, check, or proofread work
+ Work with manipulatives
+ Play games
+ Brainstorm
+ Preview and predict
+ Categorize items

- Complete graphic organizers
- Complete word sorts
- View multimedia presentations
- Share ideas and knowledge with a partner
- Write a group reflection

10-14 How to Help Groups Control Their Noise Levels

When students work together, the effectiveness of the lesson can be lost if they are so noisy that they interfere with students in other groups. Many teachers have found success with these strategies:

- Never shout. Instead, lower your voice so that students need to be quiet in order to hear you.
- Set a timer, and reward students for controlling their noise for a certain length of time.
- Reward the group with the best noise control.
- Have each group elect a noise monitor to oversee the group's noise.
- Ask for students' suggestions on how to soundproof their groups.

You can also establish signals with your students to let them know that they need to moderate their noise level:

- Flick the lights
- Fan them, so that they "chill out"
- Tell them to use a six-inch voice
- Ring a bell
- Wave your hands over your head
- Snap your fingers until students snap back
- Blow a whistle
- Play calming classical music
- Raise your hand until students raise theirs
- Clap your hands until students clap with you
- Clap twice until students clap three times
- Stand near a noisy group
- Give them a thumbs-up when they are quiet
- Give them a thumbs-down when they are noisy
- Shush the nearest group, and have them pass it on
- Place your finger over your lips, and have them do the same
- Use your "teacher look"
- Hold up your hand in a "V" for volume sign

- Games should have an educational purpose and should not be employed just to take up time. If you use them to reinforce objectives, your students will learn as they enjoy playing.

- Make sure that the games you select are suitable for your students' age, ability, maturity, and interests.

- Discourage students from becoming too competitive. Don't allow the game to become a war between boys and girls, for example. Teams should be mixed in gender and ability.

- Supervise your students when they are playing games. Be especially careful to monitor students when they are online and when they are playing games with the potential for boisterous behavior.

- Spend time teaching students the rules of good sportsmanship. Refuse to allow students to call each other names or endlessly debate the score.

- Many online games are excellent ways for students to review and recall facts.

- Before students begin playing, make sure that everyone knows the rules and procedures of the game. Try a practice game first.

- If you are not sure what types of games would appeal to your students, ask them.

- One useful way to review at the end of a unit of study is to have students create their own games and then play them with classmates.

- Games that stress teamwork instead of competition will foster a sense of community in your classroom.

10-16   Ask Questions the Right Way

- Teach the procedures you want students to follow as they answer questions you pose to the entire group. Students need to
    - Listen to their classmates' answers
    - Be respectful of each other's answers
    - Respond only when you call on them
- Allow sufficient wait time after you ask a question. Ten to fifteen seconds is usually enough.
- To engage every student, give them time to jot down their replies before raising their hands to answer.
- To keep everyone on their toes, ask a question before calling on a specific student to answer. This ensures that every student formulates a response, not just the one whose name you called.
- Many teachers have found that using a note card system makes it easy to call on every student. Draw from a stack of cards with each student's name on one card. As you run through the cards, put them back in the stack so that even those who have already answered are still held responsible for thinking and responding.
- Use open-ended questions if you want to stimulate lively discussions.
- Be careful to comment on every response. Asking students to add to each others' responses will add depth to a discussion.
- Be sure to make time for your students to ask you questions. In an active learning community, many of the questions should be student-directed.

- At the start of class, students should manage themselves as they settle to work, obtain the day's materials, and complete an anticipatory set that will focus their attention on the day's lesson.

- Many teachers have found that writing the directions for a brief opening routine in the same place each day saves time as students become accustomed to it.

- Be sure to post the objective for the day's lesson and review it at the start of class.

- Hold students accountable for the opening set by grading parts of it or asking them to share their work with classmates. Use a timer to make students aware of the need to work with purpose.

- While anticipatory sets will vary from teacher to teacher, depending on the lesson and the students, many of the ones in the following list can be adapted to different age and ability levels. Ask students to

  - Circle the homework questions or problems they would like to discuss
  - Star the homework questions or problems they are confident that they have answered correctly
  - Highlight the main points of a previous lesson
  - Respond to a passage, statement, or quotation
  - Answer a challenging question about an earlier assignment
  - Compare homework answers to correct errors
  - Copy a study skill, word, message, or problem of the day
  - Complete a brief graphic organizer
  - List what they already know about the day's lesson

10-18   Use the End of Class to Reinforce Learning

While the last two minutes of class should be allocated to having students put away their materials, tidy their work area, and gather their personal belongings, the preceding eight minutes should be devoted to review and reinforcement. Adapt the following activities to reinforce the day's learning and ensure that your students leave with positive attitudes.

Ask students to

- Play a quick review game.
- Use today's lesson to predict what they will learn in the next lesson.
- Write three things they learned, two things they found interesting, and one question they still have.
- Highlight their notes and then list the main ideas.
- Rewrite information in their own words.
- Complete an exit slip that begins
  + "I learned. . . ."
  + "I am still confused about. . . ."
  + "This lesson was valuable because. . . ."
- Share five facts with a classmate.
- Tell the class one new fact they learned. The next student must repeat that fact and add a new one until all students have had a chance to participate.
- Sketch a fact, definition, or event from the lesson.
- Write a question about the lesson. Then form two lines facing each other. Students ask the person facing them the question. After one minute of discussion, they change places with other students. After a few exchanges, they return to their seats to write out what they have learned.

☼ Brief and lively daily reviews are more productive than waiting until the night before a test to have students cram. For maximum retention, have students review information within twenty-four hours of first exposure.

☼ Solicit advice from your students about the review strategies and games that most appeal to them. When they have a voice in this decision, students will find it easier to remain on task.

☼ Before beginning a review session, ask students to determine what information they have already mastered and what they need to review, so that they can focus their efforts on new learning.

☼ Reviews should appeal to varied learning styles, just as other class activities do. Have students complete review activities that involve at least two learning modalities.

☼ Design review activities that allow students to connect new information with previous information. It is much easier to remember things that are connected than to recall isolated items.

☼ Consider adapting some of the following popular review strategies for your students. Ask students to

+ Create a quiz and give it to a classmate

+ Associate body motions with the material

+ Quiz themselves

+ Use colored pens to rewrite the main ideas

+ Recite or sing the information

+ Create mnemonic devices

+ Teach the information to a classmate

+ Create a vivid image of the topic

+ Restate information in their own words

10-20 Promote Academic Success by Teaching Study Skills

Many teachers make the mistake of assuming that someone else has taught their students how to study. To avoid this all-too-common assumption, choose one study skill each day from the following list and teach it to your students.

- Spend enough time doing your homework to do it well. Spending a few minutes looking over your notes before a test is not enough.

- Learn the material the first time you see it instead of delaying until right before a test.

- Pack your school materials at night so that all you have to do is grab them on the way out in the morning.

- At the end of an assignment, go back over your work and check it.

- Attend class. If you are absent, you miss instruction. If you have to miss, make up your work right away.

- Study the most difficult subjects first, while you are still alert.

- Use technology to help you work faster.

- Pace your work so that you don't spend so much time on one subject that you don't finish other assignments.

- Don't try to remember your homework assignment; instead, write it down.

- Pace yourself by watching the clock during an assignment that is timed.

- Do your work well the first time so you will not have to redo it.

- If you have a big project, set several early due dates so that you can get it turned in on time.

- If you have a few minutes in class, use them to review or get started on homework.

10-21 Create Helpful Study Guides

Experienced teachers know that the two most common mistakes that teachers make when creating study guides are using an advance copy of the test itself or giving students answers as well as questions. To avoid these mistakes and help your students, use the strategies in the following list.

Ask students to

- Reorganize the material by completing a graphic organizer, using their notes.
- Highlight the key information in their notes and then transfer that material to another sheet.
- Work together to predict test questions and create a study guide for them.
- Interview each other and create study guides they can share.
- Create a matching exercise or multiple-choice questions.
- Work together to brainstorm a list of questions that they predict will be on the test.
- Paraphrase or summarize information in their own words.
- Make a list of the most important facts and then check off the items on the list as they master them.
- Make a PowerPoint presentation or slide show of the material and share it with classmates.
- Create a quiz and administer it to a classmate.
- Choose questions to answer from a larger bank of possible questions.
- Make up a study guide as they work through the unit of study rather than wait until the end.
- Think outside the box! If the material lends itself, give students primary source documents, cartoons, or other interesting objects and ask them to relate the objects to the material.

CHAPTER 11

Assess Your Students' Progress

11-1   Types and Purposes of Assessments

One of the most important skills for any teacher to learn to perform competently is designing assessment instruments that are fair, accurate, and valid evaluations of student progress. Although instructional assessment is a multifaceted and sometimes difficult challenge, a sensible approach to this complicated topic is to begin by increasing your knowledge in two areas: summative assessments and formative assessments.

Summative Assessments

- The purpose of summative assessments is only to evaluate student progress or acquisition of knowledge.

- A summative assessment is not designed to provide information for the improvement of further instruction but, rather, to evaluate instruction that has already occurred.

- Examples include unit tests, final examinations, standardized tests, final projects, performance presentations, reports, and portfolios.

Formative Assessments

- The purpose of formative assessments is to provide information that can be used to adjust instruction and enhance learning. Its focus is on students' current progress.

- Countless types of formative assessments are appropriate for students of all ages and abilities. Examples include quizzes, show of hands, homework practice, questionnaires, and seatwork.

- When you have collected information from a formative assessment, ask yourself these questions in order to revise instruction:

  + How successfully is my instruction aligned with the standards and objectives for the course?

  + How can I improve the effectiveness of my teaching?

11-2 Alternative Assessments

In recent years, educators have come to appreciate the importance of *authentic assessments*—activities that engage students in assessments related to real-life content. For example, theatre students could write a review of a performance instead of just completing an objective test about stagecraft. In addition, because not all students succeed at pencil-and-paper assessments, teachers now use a wider range of assessments, including *alternative assessments,* to evaluate learning.

- Alternative assessments require that students
    - ✦ Work with the instructor in a learning partnership
    - ✦ Use problem-solving and critical thinking skills
    - ✦ Meet explicit criteria for success
    - ✦ Use self-reflection
- Here are some of the most frequently used types of alternative assessments:
    - ✦ *Holistic grading:* The work is judged on overall success rather than on specific parts.
    - ✦ *Performance assessment:* Students create slide shows, demonstrations, speeches, experiments, debates, role plays, oral reports, experiments, and projects.
    - ✦ *Group test:* All members of a group collaborate on a test together.
    - ✦ *Learning log:* Students write in a factual way about the material itself and how they engage in learning.
    - ✦ *Peer evaluation:* Students judge each other's work.
    - ✦ *Self-evaluation:* Students reflect on their own successes and failures as learners.
    - ✦ *Online assessment:* Students take quizzes and tests online instead of on paper.
    - ✦ *Case study:* Students involve themselves with one example of a particular event and report on it.
    - ✦ *Practicum:* Students complete practical work in a particular field.
    - ✦ *Class presentation:* Students teach or present material to their classmates.

11-3 How to Manage Portfolios

Portfolios offer teacher and students the opportunity to see improvement and growth over a period of time. Because portfolios are in increasingly widespread use at every grade level and because managing them can be difficult, use the following tips to learn how to handle them efficiently.

- Decide on the type of portfolio that would be most suited to your needs. There are three kinds:

  - A collection of representative, ungraded work selected by either the teacher or students that showcases various types of skills covered

  - A collection of student-selected work used to display work that students deem their most successful

  - A collection of evaluated work selected by either the teacher or students to demonstrate mastery of the material

- After you have selected the type of portfolio that would best showcase your students' work, follow these steps:

  - *Step One:* Decide

    - The purpose you want the portfolio to serve

    - The specific products that will be included

    - How long you want to maintain the portfolio

  - *Step Two:* Create a timeline of the dates when specific products are due. It is better to set periodic deadlines for small segments of work than to try to collect work all at once.

  - *Step Three:* Create a checklist for specific assignments, and include their due dates. Slip a copy of this checklist along with the criteria needed to select the work into the portfolio folder to help organize it

  - *Step Four:* Schedule the due dates on your own calendar as well as the class calendar or syllabus.

- Students should be actively involved in collecting and maintaining their portfolio. Share copies of the timeline and work with students to maintain their portfolio.

11-4 How to Create Beneficial Tests

* When you plan tests, consider these elements:
  * Format
  * Length
  * Difficulty
  * What information you need to assess
  * What types of questions will give you accurate insight into your students' progress
* Make sure that the test accurately assesses content. Write at least a rough draft of the test when you create your unit plan. Be sure the questions satisfy state objectives.
* The first questions on the test should be simple ones that build confidence.
* Use a mixture of types of questions to make it easier for all students to be successful.
* To write questions that go beyond rote memorization, use Bloom's Taxonomy as a guide to the high-level skills to assess.
* If you group questions according to their type, you will find it easier to write clear directions, grade quickly, and indicate grade point values.
* Clearly indicate the point values for each question or section so that students can estimate their grade and plan their work.
* Be careful not to go overboard on extra credit points. One bonus point question offers encouragement, whereas several may skew the final grade.
* When you design the layout, allow plenty of space and make your test easy for students to read.
* Consider how you will grade the test. It is easier to grade an answer sheet than to flip through several pages.
* Use the tests that you create to help students practice for standardized tests. Review sample questions for standardized tests, and create similar ones.

* Student-generated questions:
  + Useful for creating ownership and deeper studying
  + Work best when students generate questions throughout a unit of study
* Matching questions:
  + Useful for showing the relationships between ideas, terms, and concepts
  + Work best when matching lists are no longer than ten items in length
* Multiple-choice questions:
  + Useful for recall as well as high-level thinking skills
  + Work best when the stems and answer choices are worded carefully
* True-or-false questions:
  + Useful for recall and high-level thinking skills, but random guessing can skew results
  + Work best when students are required to explain or justify their choices
* Fill-in-the-blank questions:
  + Useful for recall of facts
  + Work best when students can draw on a word bank and statements are phrased well
* Short-answer questions:
  + Useful for recall as well as high-level thinking skills
  + Work best when students are asked to explain or interpret rather than just restate information
* Essay questions:
  + Useful for explanation and interpretation in students' own words
  + Work best when students concentrate on general concepts and new connections

11-6　The Versatile Multiple-Choice Question

Because many standardized tests rely on multiple-choice questions to assess student progress, you should provide your students with plenty of practice with this type of question. Although multiple-choice questions can be graded quickly, they can be time-consuming to create. Use the ideas listed here to reduce the time needed to create useful multiple-choice questions.

* You should use multiple-choice questions to assess complex tasks such as evaluation or application of knowledge as well as simple recall of information.

* Many teachers have found that it is easier to write questions if they first write the stem and answer as a complete statement before separating them for the final version of the test.

* Question stems can be either statements to complete or questions.

* The answer choices should appear in a single column directly below the stem and should be similar in length.

* Don't give inadvertent clues in the question. Be especially careful with plurals and the articles *a* or *an*.

* Be sure that the entire stem and the answer choices appear on the same page.

* Vary the letter pattern of the answers. Too many answers with the same letter will confuse students.

* Even though many students will just want to circle the correct answer, you will find it easier to grade multiple-choice questions if you provide a blank in the space before the stem in which students will record their answers or if you have students use an answer sheet.

One of the worst moments for any teacher is realizing that a large number of his or her students have performed poorly on a test or other summative assessment. If this happens to you and your students, you should first determine the cause of the problem. While several factors may have caused the poor performance, the two most common causes are poor assessment design and poor preparation.

Poor Assessment Design

+ Determine which part or parts of the assessment gave your students trouble.

+ After you have determined which parts of the assessment were problematic, analyze them to determine why they caused problems for your students.

+ Redesign the problematic sections, and after giving your students time to prepare again, administer the new assessment.

+ Because the first assessment instrument was faulty, do not use the grades from the first assessment, but do grade the improved one.

Poor Student Preparation

+ Discuss the situation with students to determine why students were poorly prepared.

+ Allow students to have a strong voice in determining how they will rectify their mistakes. When you take this approach, you solve the problem and treat students respectfully at the same time.

+ Design a new assessment, and allow students who did poorly to take it. You can either combine the new and old grades or use only the second grade.

11-8 Constant Informal Assessment

Constant informal assessment is a formative assessment technique that teachers use to develop an awareness of their students' grasp of material and to adjust their teaching style accordingly. To hone your informal assessment skills and help your students succeed, adapt some of these suggestions:

- Pay attention to body language. Your students telegraph both negative and positive reactions through their body language.

- Don't ask, "Are there any questions?" Instead, ask students to write one thing that they are not sure about and share it with the class.

- As you move about the room while your students are working independently, ask individuals to tell you one question they have about their work.

- Ask students to restate the directions or an important concept.

- Have students circle the question or problem that they are most unsure about. They can also mark the ones that they are confident about.

- Begin class by asking students to complete sentences such as these: "I was wondering . . ." or "I am not sure about . . ." or "I understand . . ."

- Ask students to rate their knowledge of a topic on a scale of 1 to 5.

- Pass out stickers, and have students place them beside their best and worst answers.

- Ask students to predict their grades before an assignment. Use their predictions to discuss concerns.

Gone are the days when teachers covered papers with countless terse corrections in an attempt to catch every mistake their students made. Today's teachers understand the importance of giving constructive feedback designed to help students learn from mistakes. To provide the best possible feedback for your students, try these suggestions:

- Remember that the intention of constructive feedback is not to catch students' mistakes but to help them learn through your comments.

- Be specific. Comments such as "Try changing the order of these steps" are much more helpful than "Wrong!"

- For students to gain the maximum benefit, feedback needs to be prompt. Return papers as quickly as you can, and be sure to allow time for students to review your comments and ask questions.

- Try a strategy that many teachers find useful when there are numerous errors in a class's entire set of papers: allow students to correct their work, following the directions you provide in oral comments to the class, and then regrade the papers.

- Provide a rubric at the start of an assignment and refer to it throughout the work process so that students can have a clear idea of how their final product will be evaluated.

- Useful feedback can consist of comments such as these: suggestions for change, pointed questions, specific references to things the student has done well, questions that require the student to weigh choices, or encouragement.

- Limit the number of comments you make so that you do not overwhelm your students. It is better to offer four or five helpful suggestions than to point out twenty mistakes.

11-10 Strategies for Student Success on Standardized Tests

Your goal for standardized tests should be preparing students who are confident, successful test takers who view a test as a challenging opportunity to show off their knowledge. Follow these suggestions to make your goal a reality for you and your students.

- Thoroughly familiarize yourself with the test's format and content. You will find this information on the Web site of your state's department of education.

- Teach test-taking strategies that are appropriate to your content area, as well as general ones such as these:

  - Previewing questions
  - Underlining key information in question stems
  - Following directions
  - Highlighting key words
  - Bubbling answers correctly, if the test is on paper
  - Answering easy questions first
  - Using the process of elimination
  - Double-checking answers

- Give a variety of assessments so that your students will be used to taking different types of tests. Include some questions that are in the same format as standardized test questions.

- Build your students' confidence with plenty of practice throughout the year. Begin with sessions that are brief and easy, and gradually increase the difficulty and length of each session in order to build test-taking stamina.

- Plan early how you will make accommodations for students who require them.

- If your students will use a computer to take standardized tests, make sure that they are familiar with that process.

- Teach your students some techniques for controlling test anxiety, such as deep breathing and visualization.

11-11   Attitudes That Will Help You Keep Testing in Perspective

High-stakes testing can result in excessive stress levels if you do not learn to manage the responsibilities that come with standardized tests. Many teachers have found that adopting positive, proactive attitudes about testing make it easier to keep standardized tests in perspective and reduce harmful stress.

- Work hard to be a good teacher every day. Teaching well will help you to feel confident that your students will perform well on standardized tests.

- Make test preparation part of the everyday business of your class instead of a time-consuming event several weeks before the testing date.

- Instead of dwelling on the negative aspects of testing, determine how being held accountable for your students' learning has improved your teaching.

- Accept responsibility for the part of the test that you can control and prepare your students for that, reminding yourself that you are also responsible for the entire instructional performance of your students, not just their performance on the test.

- Remind yourself that standardized tests do not drive your curriculum; state standards and guidelines do.

- Students will vary in the way that they respond to tests. Accept that some of your students will do well and that others may not be as successful.

- Don't go overboard in your attempts to scare students about tests. Help them deal with test anxiety, and focus on achievement instead.

- Remind yourself that preparing your students for standardized tests is just part of what you accomplish each day.

11-12 Keeping Up with Grading Paperwork

- Schedule time each day to take care of grading paperwork.

- Save time by using an electronic grade book.

- When you create assignments, give thought to how you will grade them.

- Return papers as soon as possible. Try to return them within three days.

- Stagger deadlines and assign a reasonable amount of work, so that you don't overwhelm your students or yourself.

- Even though it may save you time, it is not a good idea to have students grade each other's work. Proofreading and editing are acceptable, but actual grading is not.

- You do not have to grade every paper. You can still have an accurate idea of your students' growth if you try these ideas:

  - Grade a sampling of questions or problems in an assignment.

  - Have students select their best work out of several assignments for you to grade.

  - Have students check their own work.

  - Grade some assignments only for completeness.

- It is easier to grade papers with only a few errors. Have students look over each other's papers before turning them in to you.

- When students are working on an assignment with a rough draft, do not grade the draft. Check it, and make comments.

- When you make an assignment, give students the rubric that you will use to evaluate it, so that they know what they have to do to succeed.

Section Four
Look to the Future

The twenty-first century has already seen many changes in education. From the sweeping reforms of the No Child Left Behind Act to the excitement generated by the increasing integration of technology to enhance instruction, rapid change in the education profession has already had a serious impact on the lives of teachers everywhere. In this section, you will learn about some of the newest issues facing twenty-first century teachers.

CHAPTER TWELVE provides information on issues such as how to teach English language learners; teachers' increasing responsibility for teaching literacy skills; expectations under the No Child Left Behind Act; and how to deal with gangs. You will also find information about concepts that are becoming widely accepted, such as project-based learning, Howard Gardner's theory of multiple intelligences, and constructivism, and how to use those concepts to make learning in your classroom a dynamic experience.

CHAPTER 12

Twenty-First Century Issues for All Teachers

Because millions of students across the nation can be classified as English language learners, the view that schools have a responsibility to teach students whose first language is not English has significant implications for all classroom teachers. As a teacher of students who are learning English as a second language (ESL) you will be expected to

- Establish realistic expectations for academic success for ESL students.

- Help your students acquire English language skills appropriate for their age and ability.

- Create opportunities for ESL students to succeed in learning language as well as content.

- Be flexible and open-minded as you design and deliver instruction.

- Simplify and adapt material so that the language is easier for ESL learners to understand.

- Build background knowledge of language as well as content.

- Provide appropriate accommodations for students who do not learn as quickly as others.

- Help students master content knowledge at the same level of proficiency as other students.

- Use a variety of techniques, including critical thinking exercises, cooperative learning strategies, and hands-on activities.

- Help students adjust to the tensions of a bicultural life. Many of them will experience one culture at home and another at school.

- Make an effort to overcome barriers of language and culture by reaching out to the families of ESL students.

- Create a learning environment in which diversity is welcomed and cultural differences are celebrated.

The proliferation of nonprint media has caused educators to become alarmed at the nationwide increase in illiteracy. One result of this concern is the realization that all teachers share responsibility for helping students learn to read well and that it is possible for all students, even older ones, to improve their proficiency. As a literacy teacher, you will be expected to

- Teach students how to use reading strategies such as paraphrasing, summarizing, and using context clues to unlock content

- Build background knowledge through exposure to new information and experiences so that students have a context for their reading

- Use authentic informational materials so that students can apply their skills in real-life situations

- Work in partnership with the families of students to offer support, strategies, and materials for home practice

- Expose students to a variety of texts and to a variety of activities using those texts

- Use activities before, during, and after students read a passage to help them understand it

- Include comprehension and vocabulary-building skills in the daily routines of your class

- Teach students to skim, preview, and scan passages and to adjust their reading rates for various types of reading

- Employ auditory experiences that enhance reading proficiency, such as audiotapes, reading aloud, and pronunciation practice

- Use techniques such as word walls and personal dictionaries to make your classroom rich in print

12-3   The No Child Left Behind Act

The No Child Left Behind Act (NCLB) is a law that is designed to close the gap between the highest and lowest achievers in schools across the United States. Enacted in 2002, its goal is to ensure that by 2013, all students will function at grade level in math and reading. Because NCLB affects all teachers, you will be expected to

- Meet the requirements for "highly qualified" status:
    - ✦ Hold a bachelor's degree
    - ✦ Be certified to teach your course
    - ✦ Demonstrate competency through your college course work or by passing a statewide test for teachers
- Keep abreast of the changes in the law and how those changes affect your students and your school. You must acquaint yourself with your responsibilities under this law.
- Familiarize yourself with the grade-level and course standards your students must master to meet the yearly benchmarks established by your state.
- Align instruction to mandated standards to ensure that your students will pass state tests.
- Use instructional best practices to teach. You are expected to participate in various types of professional development activities designed to help you develop instruction that incorporates best practices.
- Work with students to help them successfully pass state standardized tests. You must become familiar with the test, the test content, and the strategies that students should use to pass successfully.
- Forge a strong partnership with the parents or guardians of your students as required by NCLB. You will need to use a variety of ways to reach out to them, and you will need to keep accurate documentation of your efforts.

12-4 Project-Based Learning

Project-based learning (PBL) is an instructional method that invites students to consider a real-life problem and, using various technologies, investigate the issue in collaborative groups in order to generate solutions or information. The result of their research and collaboration is presented in a final product or presentation. In PBL, students are much more self-directed than in traditional teacher-led instruction. As a teacher using PBL strategies, you will be expected to

- Help students generate questions that will motivate their investigation
- Establish cooperative groups and set deadlines for various activities
- Teach students how to use applicable research methods and technology
- Promote collaboration among students
- Coordinate ideas and materials with other teachers in an interdisciplinary approach to learning
- Guide students as they make decisions about their work
- Create a sense of shared responsibility for the project
- Ask probing questions along the way to assist students as they refine their research, make decisions, and create the final product
- Help students learn to use the technology tools that are a necessary component of PBL
- Use your own knowledge of the topic and research methods to guide students
- Help students apply the skills and information necessary for their project to work in real-life situations
- Build a solid relationship with students in your role as co-learner
- Provide direct assessment as well as opportunities for other types of evaluation such as student self-reflection and peer evaluation

12-5   Laptops for All

One of the most exciting educational innovations of recent years is the movement toward replacing computer labs with personal laptops for every student. As more schools integrate this practice, teachers with laptop classrooms experience the advantages as well as the drawbacks of this increased use of technology. In a laptop classroom, you will be expected to

- Require that students follow district policies for acceptable computer use
- Teach students the procedures for routine maintenance and care of their laptop
- Be flexible in the types of instruction and activities that you assign
- Take an active part in learning and implementing best practices for classroom computer use
- Teach students the procedures for using their laptops for academic business as opposed to personal business
- Monitor student laptop use carefully through a variety of methods, including desk arrangements, monitoring, and awareness of inappropriate content
- Teach students the procedures to ensure their personal safety when they work online
- Design lessons that use laptops as a tool to enhance instructional activities
- Provide Internet reference resources such as dictionaries or thesauruses
- Teach students how to use critical thinking skills to evaluate the usefulness and reliability of Internet sites
- Develop high-interest lessons that take advantage of the wealth of available Internet resources
- Teach students how to avoid plagiarism and other online cheating

12-6　The Internet as a Teaching Resource

Few professions have benefited from the exponential growth of the Internet as much as education. Teachers who once worked in isolation now have quick access to enormous resources. Learning how to make the best use of these resources is an important factor in teacher effectiveness. As a twenty-first century educator, you will be expected to

- Learn about and honor copyrights that apply to Internet materials.

- Use sound judgment when selecting resources for students.

- Use the Internet as just one of many effective tools for instruction.

- Be careful that the material you find is appropriate for the age and ability of your students.

- Be careful to adjust material to fit the needs of your students— for example, when you access information such as lesson plans. Follow your school's policy for acceptable use of the Internet.

- Stay current on new Web sites and other Internet resources. Try wikis and podcasts to make your instruction relevant to today's world.

Here are just a few of the resources for teachers that you can investigate on the Internet:

- Lesson plans
- Rubrics
- Online grading systems
- Clip art
- Activities
- Blogs
- New teaching strategies
- Illustrations
- Articles for students to read
- Practice exercises

- Virtual museums
- Translations
- Dictionaries
- Fact checkers
- Games
- Classroom decorations
- Videos
- Cartoons

12-7 The Theory of Multiple Intelligences

In 1983, Howard Gardner's landmark book *Frames of Mind* introduced the theory that there are various categories of human intelligence. As more and more teachers have realized the impact that instruction appealing to their students' multiple intelligences can have, the practice has become standard in today's classrooms. In order to integrate this theory into your instructional practices, you will be expected to create activities and use resources that teach to the various intelligences. Use this brief list to assist you in creating activities for each type of intelligence.

- **NATURALISTIC:** Provide activities that connect science and real life, involve students with nature, and focus on patterns.

- **INTERPERSONAL:** Provide opportunities for students to join groups, cooperate, and play games with others.

- **VISUAL/SPATIAL:** Provide opportunities for students to draw, use their imagination, and learn from videos.

- **VERBAL/LINGUISTIC:** Provide activities in which students read, write, debate, and read books and stories.

- **INTRAPERSONAL:** Provide activities that allow students to work alone, pursue their own interests, and make personal choices.

- **MUSICAL:** Provide opportunities for students to listen to music, sing, work while music is playing, and beat out rhythms.

- **BODILY/KINESTHETIC:** Provide activities that allow students to build, move, dance, use tools and instruments, and learn by doing.

- **MATHEMATICAL/LOGICAL:** Provide activities in which students work with numbers, classify, use reasoning, and work with abstract concepts.

12-8   The National Board for Professional Teaching Standards

The National Board for Professional Teaching Standards (NBPTS) is a nonprofit organization whose purpose is to increase excellence among teachers. NBPTS teachers are recognized for their knowledge and skills as indicated by the successful completion of a certification process that involves the creation of an extensive portfolio and a satisfactory score on a final examination. There are many benefits for NBPTS teachers:

- Increased pay in many districts
- "Highly qualified" status under NCLB
- Improved teaching skills
- Improved student achievement

The rigorous standards set by NBPTS are ones that should apply to all teachers. If you accept the challenge of becoming an NBPTS certified teacher you will be expected to

- Learn and use strategies that engage every learner
- Collaborate with your colleagues for the good of all students
- Take part in activities that actively enhance your professional development
- Collaborate with the families of your students
- Learn best practices and the theories that have shaped education in recent years
- View yourself as a viable contributor to your school's learning community
- Use educational best practices to design instruction
- Use assessments that offer a clear view of your students' progress
- Use self-reflection to focus on improving your teaching practices
- Demonstrate content knowledge and use successful methods for teaching that content

12-9 The Theory of Constructivism

Constructivism is a philosophy of learning based on the idea that students learn better when they engage in self-directed learning activities rather than passively receive information through lecture, seatwork, or other activities focused more on the teacher's role than on student responsibility. According to this theory, learners construct new knowledge and skills based on their previous experiences. To make the best use of constructivism in your teaching practices, you will be expected to

- Assess students' prior knowledge and build background understanding on introducing new material.

- Design activities in which students are engaged in active rather than passive learning. Some examples include

  - Group work
  - Discussions
  - Projects
  - Online research projects
  - Field trips
  - Experiments

- Assume the role of collaborator and facilitator as you guide students in making careful decisions and drawing well thought-out conclusions.

- Use such coaching techniques as providing research support and offering demonstrations, models, and examples.

- Understand and appreciate each child's strengths, work habits, and interests when designing instruction and when coaching students.

- Strengthen students' skills in collaboration, research, analyzing and evaluating information, and project organization.

- Strive to strike a balance between allowing students flexibility and providing structure when you design and deliver instruction.

Although gangs have existed for hundreds of years, their infiltration into schools has alarmed educators across the nation. As a teacher, you can do much to combat the negative influence of gangs. If you want to create an environment in which the emphasis is on learning and not on gang violence, you will be expected to

- Participate in professional development programs designed to help teachers learn about rapidly changing gang culture and its effects on schools.

- Cooperate with community leaders in their attempts to combat gang activities through various activities and programs, and encourage your students to participate in various community programs, too.

- Use your role as a teacher to offer alternatives to the violent gang lifestyle. When students see that their education will benefit them more than a gang can, it will be easier for them to resist joining.

- Help students develop a sense of belonging at school rather than in a gang.

- Be aware of the signs of gang activity among your students. Gang insignia, hand signs, and graffiti are all indicators you should be alert to.

- Report gang graffiti at once. Because graffiti can indicate threats, you should first photograph it and then erase it before it leads to conflict.

- Keep yourself safe by taking all gang activity seriously. Do not attempt to deal with gang problems by yourself. Ask school officials for help.

12-11 Response to Intervention: Early Identification and Assistance for Students with Learning Difficulties

Brought about in part because of the Individuals with Disabilities Education Improvement Act (IDEA 2004), Response to Intervention (RTI) is an approach that is used to identify and assist students who struggle academically because of learning disorders. Teachers whose school districts embrace this philosophy use data collected from various types of interventions to determine the best ways to help students learn. The RTI process uses a three-tiered format:

- TIER ONE consists of sound classroom teaching practices, including benchmark testing and alignment of curriculum with standards.

- TIER TWO involves a problem-solving approach that implements interventions designed to help the child who is experiencing difficulties. Further testing determines the success of these interventions.

- TIER THREE is similar to Tier Two in that individual interventions are offered, but in Tier Three, the interventions are offered through an Individual Education Program (IEP).

Although special education teachers will work with students who are in Tier Three, RTI also has implications for general education classroom teachers. As a classroom teacher, you will be expected to

- Deliver sound instruction aligned with your state's standards and use best practices in your teaching design and delivery

- Monitor student success through benchmark testing

- Reteach, remediate, and offer other interventions to assist students who do not initially meet benchmarks

- Act quickly to refer a student who still does not meet benchmarks after assistance

- Work with your school's RTI team and the child's parents to establish an IEP for students whose response to interventions reveals that their learning disabilities require support beyond what can be offered by a general education teacher

Section Five

Helpful Resources for Educators

Being a new teacher can be thrilling, rewarding—and overwhelming. From lesson planning and assessment to meetings with staff and parents, even experienced educators need help and guidance along the way. In this section, you'll learn about the many excellent books available on the teaching profession and the scores of helpful Web sites that offer teachers a variety of educational resources.

IN CHAPTER THIRTEEN, you'll learn where to go to get information, advice, and tools on everything from classroom setup to classroom management and discipline to working well with others.

IN CHAPTER FOURTEEN, you'll discover many useful books and Web sites that will help you forge strong relationships with students and assist struggling learners.

CHAPTER 13

Resources to Help You Become a Better Teacher

* *American Federation of Teachers (AFT).* The AFT, a teachers' union allied with the AFL-CIO, has been a strong voice supporting classroom teachers for decades. (www.aft.org)

* *Association for Supervision and Curriculum Development (ASCD).* This group is a nonprofit national and international organization for educators at all grade levels. (www.ascd.org)

* *National Association for the Education of Young Children (NAEYC).* This group is the nation's largest organization for early childhood educators. (www.naeyc.org)

* *National Board for Professional Teaching Standards (NBPTS).* This nonprofit organization's purpose is to improve teaching through voluntary certification. (www.nbpts.org)

* *National Coalition for Parental Involvement in Education (NCPIE).* Founded in 1980, NCPIE is an organization devoted to creating a partnership between parents and schools. (www.ncpie.org)

* *National Education Association (NEA).* With almost three million members, the NEA is the largest organization for public school teachers in the United States. (www.nea.org)

* *National High School Association (NHSA).* This nonprofit association is dedicated to improving the professional knowledge of high school educators. (www.nhsa.net)

* *National Middle School Association (NMSA).* NMSA is the largest national education association committed to the educational needs of middle school adolescents. (www.nmsa.org)

* *Parent Teacher Association (PTA).* The PTA is an organization whose membership consists of millions of teachers and parents who work together for the good of school children. (www.pta.org)

* *Phi Delta Kappa International (PDK).* This international organization for educators offers opportunities to network with other professional educators. (www.pdkintl.org)

13-2 Resources on Classroom Management and Discipline

Books

* Arnie Bianco. *One-Minute Discipline: Classroom Management Strategies That Work.* San Francisco: Jossey-Bass, 2002.

* Carol Bradford Cummings. *Winning Strategies for Classroom Management.* Alexandria, Va.: Association for Supervision and Curriculum Development, 2000.

* Philip S. Hall and Nancy D. Hall. *Educating Oppositional and Defiant Children.* Alexandria, Va.: Association for Supervision and Curriculum Development, 2003.

* Fredric H. Jones. *Tools for Teaching.* Santa Cruz, Calif.: Fredric H. Jones and Associates, 2000.

* Renee Rosenblum-Lowden and Felicia Lowden Kimmel. *You Have to Go to School—You're the Teacher! 300 + Classroom Management Strategies to Make Your Job Easier and More Fun.* Thousand Oaks, Calif.: Corwin Press, 2007.

* Rick Smith. *Conscious Classroom Management.* Fairfax, Calif.: Conscious Teaching Publications, 2004.

* Julia G. Thompson. *Discipline Survival Kit for the Secondary Teacher.* San Francisco: Jossey-Bass, 1998.

Web Sites

* *Intervention Central (www.interventioncentral.org).* At Intervention Central, you will find many resources and tools to promote productive classroom behaviors.

* *National Youth Violence Prevention Center (www.safeyouth.org).* Here you can learn about the effects of gangs on schools and what educators can do to cope with the problem.

* *Tolerance.org (www.tolerance.org).* At this site maintained by the Southern Poverty Law Center, you can access resources that will help you teach your students about alternatives to violence as well as how to deal with issues of racism and bigotry.

* *You Can Handle Them All (www.disciplinehelp.com).* You Can Handle Them All offers resources to help you deal successfully with the 117 most common classroom misbehaviors.

13-3 Resources to Help with Teaching, Instruction, and Lesson Planning

Books to Help You Become a Better Teacher

* Jere Brophy. *Motivating Students to Learn*. (2nd ed.) Mahwah, N.J.: Lawrence Erlbaum, 2004.

* Jim Burke. *Teacher's Essential Guide: Effective Instruction*. New York: Scholastic Teaching Resources, 2008.

* Marva Collins. *Ordinary Children, Extraordinary Teachers*. Charlottesville, Va.: Hampton Roads, 1992.

* Harvey Daniels and Marilyn Bizar. *Methods That Matter: Six Structures for Best Practice Classrooms*. Portland, Me.: Stenhouse Publishers, 1998.

* Charlotte Danielson. *Enhancing Professional Practice*. (2nd ed.) Alexandria, Va.: Association for Supervision and Curriculum Development, 2007.

* Howard Gardner. *Multiple Intelligences: New Horizons in Theory and Practice*. New York: Basic Books, 2006.

* Giselle O. Martin-Kniep. *Becoming a Better Teacher: Eight Innovations That Work*. Alexandria, Va.: Association for Supervision and Curriculum Development, 2000.

* Robert J. Marzano, Jane E. Pollock, and Debra J. Pickering. *Classroom Instruction That Works: Research-Based Strategies for Increasing Student Achievement*. Alexandria, Va.: Association for Supervision and Curriculum Development, 2001.

* Paula Rutherford. *Why Didn't I Learn This in College?* Alexandria, Va.: Just Ask Publications, 2002.

* James H. Stronge. (2nd ed.) Alexandria, Va.: Association for Supervision and Curriculum Development, 2007.

* Carol Ann Tomlinson. *How to Differentiate Instruction in Mixed-Ability Classrooms*. (2nd ed.) Alexandria, Va.: Association for Supervision and Curriculum Development, 2004.

* Todd Whitaker. *What Great Teachers Do Differently: Fourteen Things That Matter Most*. Larchmont, N.Y.: Eye on Education, 2003.

Books to Help You Create Engaging Instruction

* Denise Dodds Harrell, Barbara Hillis, Julia Jasmine, and Dona Jerweck Rice. *Jumbo Book of Teacher Tips and Timesavers.* Westminster, Calif.: Teacher Created Resources, 2004.

* Louanne Johnson. *Teaching Outside the Box: How to Grab Your Students by Their Brains.* San Francisco: Jossey-Bass, 2005.

* Alexis Ludewig and Amy Swan. *101 Great Classroom Games.* New York: McGraw-Hill, 2007.

* Patty Nelson. *Teacher's Bag of Tricks: 101 Instant Lessons for Classroom Fun.* Nashville, Tenn.: Incentive Publications, 1986.

* Kimberly Persiani-Becker, Brandy Alexander, and Steve Springer. *The Creative Teacher.* New York: McGraw-Hill, 2006.

Web Sites for Lesson Plans, Teaching Ideas, and Instructional Materials

* *A to Z Teacher Stuff (www.atozteacherstuff.com).* You will find lesson plans, articles, and much more in the thousands of pages at this large, easy-to-navigate site.

* *AskERIC (www.eric.ed.gov).* This site provides access to over a million education-related articles in the ERIC resource library.

* *Awesome Library (www.awesomelibrary.org).* At Awesome Library, you will find over 35,000 online resources for teachers at all grade levels.

* *Blue Web'n (www.kn.pacbell.com/wired/bluewebn).* Blue Web'n is an excellent online library of educational tools, lesson plans, and resources for all teachers.

* *Cool Lessons (www.coollessons.org).* Click on the "Cool Teaching Lessons and Units" box to access thousands of interesting sites for teachers and students.

* *Education Oasis (www.educationoasis.com).* At this nonprofit site created for teachers by teachers, you will find free resources and a large collection of links to other educational resources for teachers.

* *Education World (www.education-world.com).* Education World is a wide-ranging site that includes lesson plans, tutorials for teachers, information for professional development, and much more.

* *Edutopia (www.edutopia.org)*. Edutopia is a site maintained by the George Lucas Educational Foundation. Here you will learn about technology integration in the classroom as well as a variety of other current issues in education. It is a particularly useful site for learning about project-based learning activities.

* *Internet4Classrooms (www.internet4classrooms.com)*. At this large Web portal, you can find thousands of links for teachers as well as assessment assistance and online practice sites for students.

* *Julia G. Thompson (www.juliagthompson.com)*. Here you will find teaching tips, links to resources, study guides, a monthly newsletter, and more.

* *Lesson Plans Page (www.lessonplanspage.com)*. This site offers teacher discussion, news articles, more than 3,500 free lesson plans, and many other items of interest to teachers.

* *Library of Congress (www.loc.gov)*. At the Library of Congress home page, use "The Learning Page" as a search term in order to access thousands of lesson plans and other resources for teachers.

* *National Geographic (http://www.nationalgeographic.com)*. At the National Geographic site, you can find hundreds of resources to help your students learn about their world.

* *National Public Radio (www.npr.org)*. NPR offers years of archived audio information as well as noncommercial news and radio programming.

* *TeacherTube (http://teachertube.com)*. TeacherTube offers short videos on an enormous variety of topics for teachers and students.

13-4 Resources on Assessment

The following Web sites contain scores of helpful rubrics and other resources to help with assessment.

* *Chicago Public Schools Instructional Intranet (http://www.intranet.cps. k12.il.us).* On the home page for this extensive site, use "assessment" as a search term to search the various links for ideas on how to use rubrics, alternative assessments, and ways to help your students improve their standardized test performance.

* *Discovery School (http://school.discoveryeducation.com).* From the Discovery School home page, use "assessment" as a search term to access the extensive collection of rubrics, portfolio ideas, and other assessment resources.

* *RubiStar (http://rubistar.4teachers.org).* RubiStar is a very useful, free source of dozens of rubric templates that teachers can customize for their students.

* *TeacherVision (www.teachervision.fen.com).* From the home page, use "assessment" as a search term in order to access dozens of pages of advice about traditional and alternative assessments.

Here are three good books about assessment:

* Susan M. Butler and Nancy D. McMunn. *A Teacher's Guide to Classroom Assessment: Understanding and Using Assessment to Improve Student Learning.* San Francisco: Jossey-Bass, 2006.

* W. James Popham. *Classroom Assessment: What Teachers Need to Know.* (5th ed.) New York: Allyn & Bacon, 2007.

* Grant Wiggins. *Educative Assessment: Designing Assessments to Inform and Improve Student Performance.* San Francisco: Jossey-Bass, 1998.

13-5 Resources to Help with Time Management, Organization, and Workplace Skills

Books

* Michael S. Dobson and Susan B. Wilson. *Goal Setting: How to Create an Action Plan and Achieve Your Goals.* (2nd ed.) New York: AMACOM, 2008.

* Steve Springer, Brandy Alexander, and Kimberly Persiani-Becker. *The Organized Teacher.* New York: McGraw-Hill, 2005.

Web Sites

* *Mind Tools (www.mindtools.com).* This site offers resources on communication, stress management, and other career skills, in addition to time management skills.

* *Time-Management-Guide.com (www.time-management-guide.com).* This helpful site offers sensible suggestions for time management, as well as links to related sites.

* *United States Department of Education (www.ed.gov/nclb/landing.jhtml).* In this section of the U.S. Department of Education's Web site, you can learn about the requirements of the No Child Left Behind Act and how it affects your professional life.

13-6 Resources to Help You Work Well with Others

The following books offer lots of great advice and ideas for working well with parents and coworkers.

- ✳ Betty Boult. *176 Ways to Involve Parents: Practical Strategies for Partnering with Families.* (2nd ed.) Thousand Oaks, Calif.: Corwin Press, 2006.

- ✳ Matthew Gilbert. *Communication Miracles at Work: Effective Tools and Tips for Getting the Most from Your Work Relationships.* Newburyport, Mass.: Red Wheel/Weiser, 2002.

- ✳ Diana B. Hiatt-Michael. *Promising Practices for Family Involvement in Schools.* Charlotte, N.C.: Information Age Publishing, 2001.

- ✳ Mavis G. Sanders. *Building School-Community Partnerships: Collaboration for Student Success.* Thousand Oaks, Calif.: Corwin Press, 2005.

13-7 Resources for Classroom Arrangement and Decoration

These Web sites are great resources to use when setting up your classroom for the first time, creating new project-related bulletin boards, or just decorating for holidays:

* *Discovery School (http://school.discoveryeducation.com/schrockguide)*. Kathy Schrock's part of the larger Discovery School site contains an impressive list of bulletin board ideas, links, and resources.

* *Google Images (http://images.google.com)*. If you use "classroom seating arrangements" as a search word at Google Images, you can view hundreds of diagrams and photographs of classrooms.

* *Oriental Trading Company (www.orientaltrading.com)*. At Oriental Trading Company, you can shop their extensive catalogue of supplies for classroom decoration.

* *Scholastic (http://content.scholastic.com)*. Scholastic has a helpful section on its Web site that is devoted to setting up a classroom efficiently. Use "classroom organization" as a search term from the home page.

* *The Teacher's Corner (www.theteacherscorner.net)*. Here you can link to many other sites that offer ideas and supplies for bulletin boards and classroom decorations.

* *Teachnet.com (www.teachnet.com)*. At Teachnet's home page, use "word wall" as a search word to learn how to make and use word walls that will appeal to your students.

* *TeacherStorehouse.com (http://teacherstorehouse.com)*. This site offers materials for decorating your room as well as other teaching supplies.

* *TeacherVision (www.teachervision.fen.com)*. At TeacherVision, use "classroom organization" as a search term to access many different articles about the best ways to organize your classroom.

CHAPTER 14

Resources to Help You Work with Students

14-1 Resources to Help You Connect with Your Students

The following books provide valuable insights that will help you relate to your students, whatever the circumstances.

◆ Jim Fay and David Funk. *Teaching with Love and Logic.* Golden, Colo.: Love and Logic Press, 2006.

◆ Daniel Goleman. *Emotional Intelligence: Why It Can Matter More Than IQ.* (10th anniversary ed.) New York: Bantam, 2006.

◆ Jonathan Kozol. *Savage Inequities: Children in America's Schools.* New York: Harper Perennial, 1992.

◆ Allen Mendler. *Connecting with Students.* Alexandria, Va.: Association for Supervision and Curriculum Development, 2001.

◆ Ruby K. Payne. *A Framework for Understanding Poverty.* (4th ed.) Chicago: ahaPress, 2005.

◆ Kevin Ryan and Karen E. Bohlin. *Building Character in Schools: Practical Ways to Bring Moral Instruction to Life.* San Francisco: Jossey-Bass, 2003.

14-2 Resources on Helping Students with Special Needs

Books

◆ Mimi Gold. *Help for the Struggling Student: Ready-to-Use Strategies and Lessons to Build Attention, Memory, and Organizational Skills.* San Francisco: Jossey-Bass, 2003.

◆ Joan M. Harwell and Rebecca Williams Jackson. *The Complete Learning Disabilities Handbook: Ready-to-Use Strategies and Activities for Teaching Students with Learning Disabilities.* (3rd ed.) San Francisco: Jossey-Bass, 2008.

◆ Constance McGrath. *The Inclusion-Classroom Problem Solver: Structures and Supports to Serve All Learners.* Portsmouth, N.H.: Heinemann, 2007.

◆ Roger Pierangelo. *The Special Educator's Survival Guide.* San Francisco: Jossey-Bass, 2004.

◆ Sandra Rief. *How to Reach and Teach All Children in the Inclusive Classroom: Practical Strategies, Lessons, and Activities.* (2nd ed.) San Francisco: Jossey-Bass, 2006.

◆ Judy Willis. *Brain-Friendly Strategies for the Inclusion Classroom.* Alexandria, Va.: Association for Supervision and Curriculum Development, 2007.

Organizations

◆ *Children and Adults with Attention-Deficit/Hyperactivity Disorder (CHADD).* This nonprofit organization is the nation's leading advocacy group for children and adults with attention disorders. (www.chadd.org)

◆ *Council for Exceptional Children (CEC).* CEC is the nation's largest advocacy organization for children with exceptionalities such as gifted children and children with disabilities. (www.cec.sped.org)

◆ *Recording for the Blind and Dyslexic.* Recording for the Blind and Dyslexic is a nonprofit group that offers audio recordings of various types of books, including textbooks. (www.rfbd.org)

Web Sites

◆ *Dave's ESL Café (www.eslcafe.com).* Dave Sperling offers an abundance of information for teachers of students who are English language learners as well as hundreds of activities and games of interest to every teacher.

◆ *LdPride.net (www.ldpride.net).* At this useful site devoted to students with learning disabilities, you will find a learning styles inventory as well as a great deal of information about multiple intelligences and children with disabilities.

◆ *LoudLit.org (http://loudlit.org).* Hundreds of public domain literary works in audio form are ready to be downloaded at no cost.

◆ *National Center on Response to Intervention (www.rti4success.org).* At the National Center on Response to Intervention site you can learn more about the innovative Response to Intervention program and access a library, tools, interventions, and discussion forums.

◆ *U.S. Department of Education (www.ed.gov).* At the U.S. Department of Education's Web site, you will find hundreds of articles and resources on helping students with special needs. Use "students with special needs" as a search term on the home page.

Books

◆ Gail Boushey and Joan Moser. *The Daily Five: Fostering Literacy Independence in the Elementary Grades*. Portland, Me.: Stenhouse Publishers, 2006.

◆ Jim Burke. *Reading Reminders, Tools, Tips, Techniques*. Portsmouth, N.H.: Boynton/Cook, 2000.

◆ Stephanie Harvey and Anne Goudvis. *Strategies That Work: Teaching Comprehension for Understanding and Engagement*. Portland, Me.: Stenhouse Publishers, 2007.

◆ Chris Tovani. *Do I Really Have to Teach Reading? Content Comprehension, Grades 6–12*. Portland, Me.: Stenhouse Publishers, 2004.

Web Sites

◆ *Center for the Study of Reading (http://csr.ed.uiuc.edu)*. The Center for the Study of Reading conducts research and provides much useful information about reading practices for educators.

◆ *Educational Development Center (www.literacymatters.org)*. Here you can learn much about how to help students in middle and secondary grades learn to read with greater skill. This useful site has extensive links to the latest information on reading and literacy for adolescent readers.

◆ *International Reading Association (www.reading.org)*. The International Reading Association is an influential organization of literacy professionals. At their Web site, you will find extensive information about literacy issues.

Index

The First-Year Teacher's Survival Guide

Ready-to-Use Strategies, Tools & Activities for
Meeting the Challenges of Each School Day

2ⁿᵈ Edition

By: JULIA G. THOMPSON

ISBN 978-0-7879-9455-6
Paperback | 464 pp.

"Every new teacher of the twenty-first century needs this book! Julia Thompson has skillfully created an invaluable survival guide filled with a wealth of expertise and wisdom to help new teachers through almost every problem they may encounter." —**Sherry Cameron**, sixth-grade resource teacher, Richard B. Wilson K–8 School, Tucson, Arizona

"...Thompson uses her own expertise and high standards to show novice professionals how they can not just survive, but thrive. Best of all, her own love of her students shines on every page."—**Margaret Hallau**, director, National Outreach, Research, and Evaluation Network at the Laurent Clerc National Deaf Education Center, Gallaudet University

"This book should be mandatory reading for all beginning teachers! Julia Thompson has created an invaluable resource that will empower new teachers with its wealth of practical information, classroom-proven strategies, and wise advice." —**Robin Gardner**, Uniserv director, Virginia Education Association, Richmond, Virginia

The completely revised and updated edition of the best-selling *First-Year Teacher's Survival Kit* offers beginning teachers a wide variety of tested strategies, activities, and tools for creating a positive and dynamic learning environment while meeting the challenges of each school day. The book is filled with valuable tips, suggestions, and ideas for helping teachers with everything from becoming effective team players and connecting with students to handling behavior problems and working within diverse classrooms.

Discipline Survival Kit for the Secondary Teacher

By: JULIA G. THOMPSON

ISBN 978-0-87628-434-6
Paperback | 384 pp.

This unique, hands-on resource is packed with tested ideas and strategie to help you create a classroom environment where good conduct and hig achievement are the norm – where students become self-motivated an take responsibility for their actions – and where you experience th satisfaction that only a career in education can bring!

Discipline Survival Kit is a practical, hands-on resource packed wit tested tips, techniques, tools, and activities such as "27 Power-Packe Time-Management Tips for Students," "Monitoring On the Run: 20 Quic Techniques," "Missing Work Reminder List," and "50 Sponge Activitie to Keep Students Engaged in Learning All Period Long."

For easy use, the *Discipline Survival Kit* is organized into nine key are of classroom management and printed in a big 8 ½ by 11-inch format fc photocopying the scores of full-page forms, checklists, and other ready-tc use tools throughout.

In the author's own words, *"Without a mannerly classroom environmen no lesson, no matter how creative, how beautifully planned, or ho artfully delivered, can be successful. There are many ways to help studen learn to be successful while managing their own actions."* You'll fir hundreds of them in this resource.